COMMANDER'S GUIDE

THIS IS A CARLTON BOOK

This edition published by Carlton Books Limited
20 Mortimer Street
London W1T 3JW

Editorial Director: Roland Hall
Editorial consultant: Nick Johnston
Design Manager: James Pople
Production: Lisa French
Picture Research: Steve Behan

WORLD OF TANKS

ROLL OUT

COMMANDER'S GUIDE

CONTENTS

ACKNOWLEDGEMENTS

All World of Tanks, World of Warplanes and World of Warships images and logos copyright © 2015 Wargaming.net

www.worldoftanks.com

www.worldofwarplanes.com

www.worldofwarships.com

All photographs supplied by The Tank Museum: www.tankmuseum.org

INTRODUCTION

I first heard of World of Tanks as the punchline of a joke. It was 2011 and although the game had been wildly successful in Russia we in the West were only just hearing about it. Back then the phrase "World of" was nearly always followed by "Warcraft", so once press releases about "World of Tanks" started dropping in journalist inboxes we just couldn't resist picturing adorable little tanks going on quests, killing ten boars, collecting loot and raiding dungeons. Being game journalists we, of course, felt compelled to share these silly little jokes with the world, and a meme was born. In many ways, I wonder if the incessant lighthearted ridicule may have helped. After all, every silly line about questing in the Level One tank zone was another bit of coverage for the game.

Then, after a couple of weeks of terrible puns, we finally settled down and noticed something: the game was actually very good. It was neither a comedy MMO nor an overcomplicated simulation, but actually boiled the complex act of tank warfare down to a simple, easy to control shooter. It was immediately compelling in a way no other tank-based game had ever managed to acheive.

I was one of the first journalists to check it out. Naturally I figured I'd make things easier for myself by recruiting a friend, and expert, to show me the ropes. Thus I clambered into my starter tank, the Leichttraktor, grouped up with my friend and queued for a match.

Experienced players reading this will already know where I went wrong.

World of Tanks matchmaking is usually very good, especially these days, but back in 2011 the team of a top tier veteran and a guy in his first ever game was just too much for it to handle. I found myself in a high level deathmatch in a vehicle I would later find out the community affectionately refers to as "The Loltraktor". Now you'd think

these grizzled veterans would dismiss me as no threat, but you'd be wrong. Almost immediately the chat exploded with people crying "Kill the Tier I!" The original match objectives were rapidly forgotten – killing me was the priority!

Tanks three times my size smashed through walls and ran clean through houses, quite literally clambouring over one another for the honour of being the first to kill me. Meanwhile, my own puny shots bounced right off the armour of every tank present. I was completely outclassed. Yet somehow I managed to find respite, using my small size to hide myself behind a derelict farmhouse. Moments later I exploded. I would realize later I'd been hit by an artillery shot. The driver must have eschewed the many slow moving, vulnerable, high value targets in favour of destroying me with a shell that cost more than my entire tank! The Loltraktor's moment in the sun ended suddenly.

It was a rather short, uneventful game in which I achieved nothing, but nevertheless I had caught the bug. Seeing those armoured behemoths crash straight through stone walls in an attempt to slaughter the least threatening vehicle on the field had convinced me that this was a game worth trying. I quickly jumped into a new tank and began playing again, this time without accidentally breaking the matchmaking system in half. I played regularly for the next few weeks, writing about it occasionally for the magazine I worked for. It was not long after this that I was sent down to a local tank show to interview Victor Kislyi about the game and hear his own account of how it all began. I wrote the interview on the train home and filed it the next day. I've been playing and writing about World of Tanks ever since.

Those years have given me a lot of great anecdotes, such as the time I first saw a T2 light tank, capable of an astonishing 72 kph, coming straight for me. The driver had realized speed was his greatest weapon, and had

abandoned all attempt at fighting in favour of making a huge circuit around the entire field, building up as much momentum as possible before ramming a self-propelled gun in a spectacular fireball. I was also playing the day the game switched physics engines, witnessing the chaos that happens when a game suddenly changes from it being impossible to fall off the edge of a cliff, to it being not only possible but happening *all the time*, as players gleefully rammed one another or tried high speed leaps! I even once experienced an entire team mass buy the comically slow and oversized TOG II, just before the match, as a joke.

Those years have afforded me a lot of time to think about why exactly World of Tanks works. I think the key is surface simplicity. The game takes the complicated nature of tank battles, elements such as angled plating and gun depression, and hides it all behind an incredibly accessible third person shooter interface. If you've played a shooter before, you can immediately pick up and play World of Tanks. In terms of controls it's similiar to playing Call of Duty, only with a soldier that weighs 26-tons and can smash through houses. All the complex simulations of shell calibre and armour thickness are still happening, but they're in the background and you don't have to engage with them until you've mastered the basics.

Then there's the free-to-play aspect. Hard as it may seem now, that was a tough sell in the West back in 2011. It was too associated with Facebook games and low budget MMOs (even the mobile free-to-play craze was just beginning). World of Tanks, along with League of Legends and Team Fortress 2, helped bring free-to-play into the mainstream. It was one of the first free-to-play games I'd ever seen grace the cover of a gaming magazine, and it was also the first that didn't rely on a pre-existing fanbase. So many titles had come over from the East and failed to find a footing, but World of Tanks succeeded because, ultimately, it felt fair in a way the early free-to-play games never had. Soon major publishers would be flirting with the concept of free-to-play games themselves.

So, now you know what World of Tanks is and why I love it, let me answer the more pressing question: what is this book and why are you reading it? Well, consider it a guide to your first steps (or rather first drive) into the world of the tank commander. When I visited one of Wargaming's events at the The Tank Museum in Bovington, I saw a wildly diverse fanbase. Sure, there was the traditional gaming audience, but there were also children and military enthusiasts, people from outside the gaming world but who simply loved really big tanks and other mighty metal machines.

This book is for all those people. The hope is that it will help you get to grips with the game a little quicker. That's not to say that you can't jump right into World of Tanks, in fact you can do it right now! Get right in that starter tank and play a match. Go on, I'll wait.

Okay, done that? You probably got blown to smithereens, didn't you? This is where the book comes in. Hopefully I'll be able to take you step-by-step from winning your first starter match to hanging out in the mid-tier, to fighting as part of a large clan. (But if you simply want to get better at that first match right away, turn now to page 28).

Consider this book a condensed version of the four year journey I've taken, plus a little bit further, with information sourced from friends of mine involved in high level competitive matches. Within these pages I'm going to break down every aspect of the game: Tech Trees, Crew Management and experience, plus a spotlight on some of my favourite tanks. Alongside that I'll also be bringing you as many tips and tactics as possible, from how to get better at your first match, to map specific strategies all the way up to Tier X and how to master clan warfare. Finally, I'll be bringing you a little information on the reality behind the game, with insights into the history of tank warfare and a gallery of real world tanks provided by our good friends at The Tank Museum in Bovington.

Are you ready? Let's fire up those engines...

HISTORY OF TANKS

Like many of Leonardo Da Vinci's creations, the tank was too ingenious for its time. With no internal combustion engine Da Vinci would have had to rely on strong men turning cranks, which would have left his design chronically underpowered.

Da Vinci may have been the first to imagine great armoured vehicles, but he was not the last. For centuries artists and authors speculated about tank-like vehicles. One of the last and most accurate came from H.G. Wells, whose 1903 short story "The Land Ironclads" depicted huge ship like vehicles crawling across the landscape on pedrail wheels (an early forerunner to tracks). Only 12 years later his dream would come true.

The key ingredient that both Wells and Da Vinci were lacking was the caterpillar track, which made it possible for the bulk of a tank to be spread across rough ground, making large all-terrain vehicles a possibility. In 1914, with World War I stuck in trench warfare stalemate, armed forces officers began lobbying for armoured vehicles to break the deadlock. Eventually Winston Churchill founded the Landships Committee to begin investigating the concept. The result was a prototype called 'Little Willie'. Its primary purpose was to drive across no-man's land while shielding infantry from fire. Speed and firepower came a distant second to armour and all terrain ability.

Little Willie still survives today in The Tank Museum in Bovington. It never actually saw combat as it was found to have trouble crossing trenches. Instead, a second prototype dubbed 'Big Willie' or 'Mother' was created, and became the basis for the Type 1 tank. There is some disagreement over where the name 'tank' came from, although the popular legend is that landships were referred to as 'water tanks' to keep their existence a secret from German spies.

After the first wave of British prototypes other nations began experimenting with early tank designs. The most influential foundation came from the French who developed the Renault FT, the first tank to sport what would become the standard configuration for tanks today: engine to the rear, crew compartment at the front and, most importantly, a fully rotating turret. The FT was an enormous success, with the French producing 3,000 by the end of World War I.

During World War I the prevailing philosophy was that there were two kinds of tank. Type 1s and their descendants were considered heavy or 'infantry' tanks. They were heavily armed and armoured but travelled at walking pace, designed to break enemy lines, cross trenches and shield infantry from attacks. Meanwhile, the FT and later designs – such as the British Whippet – were considered light tanks,

....

Left: The world's first tank, Little Willie. It never entered full production but the prototype resides at the Tank Museum in Bovington.

Below: Leonardo da Vinci came up with an armoured fighting vehicle in 1487. The famous shape was inspired by a turtle's shell.

or 'cavalry' tanks. They were used much as horsemen had been before World War I, using their speed to exploit gaps in the enemy lines. Both were expected to largely engage infantry or fortifications, and it wasn't until 1918 that the first tank on tank engagement occurred.

This conventional wisdom went largely unchallenged until the outbreak of World War II, and the advent of *blitzkrieg*: the lightning war. When Germany invaded France in 1940 the French possessed a large tank force, including some extremely potent heavy tanks whose armour the German forces struggled to penetrate. However, many of these were 'infantry tanks' that lacked speed and were assigned to protect foot infantry rather than forming their own divisions. Furthermore many of them lacked radios, making it even harder for them to rapidly reinforce one another. As a result the Germans were able to simply outmanoeuvre the French forces, bypassing their fortified defences and simply electing not to fight the formidable French heavy tanks. The backbone of this German assault were the Panzer III and Panzer IV. They were medium tanks, sporting thick enough armour to deflect light anti-tank weapons, a large enough gun to challenge other tanks and enough engine power to keep up with the rest of the army. They were often accompanied by mechanized infantry, and they would become the blueprint for the rest of the war.

Two of the most important tanks of World War II were the Soviet T-34 and the American M4 Sherman. Neither was the best tank of the war, indeed both were outmatched by the late-war German Panther and Tiger tanks. Instead, they represented a fair compromise between speed, armour, firepower and most importantly cost. Both were eminently mass producible, allowing them to simply outnumber the costlier German tanks. In addition, their chassis could also easily be adapted in order to upgrade the main gun or refit them to suit a variety of battlefield roles.

Despite the tide starting to turn in favour of the more manoeuvrable medium tanks heavy tanks, such as the Tiger, Tiger II and IS-2, continued to be produced. Indeed the late war saw the Germans experiment with superheavy tanks and heavily armoured tank destroyers. This was likely more a result of Hitler's love of gigantic tanks than any practical battlefield requirement, with many German generals privately doubting their usefulness. Many of these took the form of small production runs, such as the

unreliable Jagdtiger, or experimental prototypes, such as the Panzer VIII Maus, of which only two were developed before being captured by the allies. Very few superheavy tanks would be developed after the war, with nations instead investing in the medium tank.

This mass use of tanks also caused both sides to experiment with dedicated tank destroyers. Equipped with oversized guns at the expense of versatility, tank destroyers existed to annihilate enemy armour and could accomplish little else, often attacking from ambush or defensive positions. As a result the vast majority of tank destroyers did not have turrets like traditional tanks, giving them a lower profile, for stealth, and reducing the weight requirement to carry their oversized guns. Early tank destroyers, such as the Marder II, were created by simply mounting a static anti-tank gun on a convenient tracked or wheeled platform. Later developments would use modular tank chassis, with the lack of a turret and emphasis on ambush allowing designers to incorporate thicker armour. Tank destroyers achieved mixed results over the course of the war, as

they required a significant amount of forethought and planning to use. The U.S. created entire tank destroyer companies as a counter to massed German tanks, only to find themselves faced with combined armed forces instead. By the 1960s the concept of the tank destroyer had been completely abandoned as a result of the increased use of anti-tank missiles.

By the end of World War II, and the beginning of the Cold War, it was clear that times had changed. The old light/heavy specialization had been jettisoned. As engine and armour technlogy became more powerful, it became increasingly possible to have strong armour, high speed and devastating firepower all at once. The late-war Cromwell tank in particular was notable for having firepower comparable to an 'infantry' tank, but the speed of a 'cruiser'. Eventually it would be replaced with the Centurion, a wildly successful post-war tank design that excelled in every area. Thus began the era of universality, specializations were out... and the "Main Battle Tank" was in.

....

Below: The British Mk I tank, photographed in 1916. Note the anti-grenade frame with mesh on top and the steering tail, here raised.

TANK TIMELINE

1914 World War I begins

1914 Concept of the 'landship' first proposed, Winston Churchill is an early proponent

1915 Little Willie is created

1916 The first Mk I tanks are produced and see combat at The Somme, Ypres and Amiens

1917 Renault FT developed, creating the standard design for future tanks

1917 Tanks are decisive in the Battle of Cambrai, but the breakthrough is not properly exploited

1918 The first tank vs tank battle takes place at the battle of Villers-Bretonneux

1918 World War I ends

1926 Defying the treaty of Versailles, Germany begins to develop tanks

1937 Panzer III and IV developed, they will form the backbone of Germany's early war forces and prove the effectiveness of medium tanks

1939 World War II begins

1940 The German invasion of France showcases new tank tactics

1941 Germany invades the USSR, prompting mass production of the T-34, one of the most important tanks of the war

1942 Germany develops the Tiger heavy tank to compete with the T-34

1942 America develops the M4 Sherman. It will be used extensively by both the U.S. and UK

1943 The Battle of Kursk – the largest tank battle in history – is fought

1943 Germany develops the Panther and Tiger II (1944). They are superior to the T-34 and M4 Sherman, but cannot be mass-produced as easily

1944 USSR produced the IS-2 as a counter to German Tigers

1944 The prototype Panzer VIII Maus is produced and swiftly captured by the allies

1945 World War II ends

1946 The Centurion, the first Main Battle Tank, is created in the UK

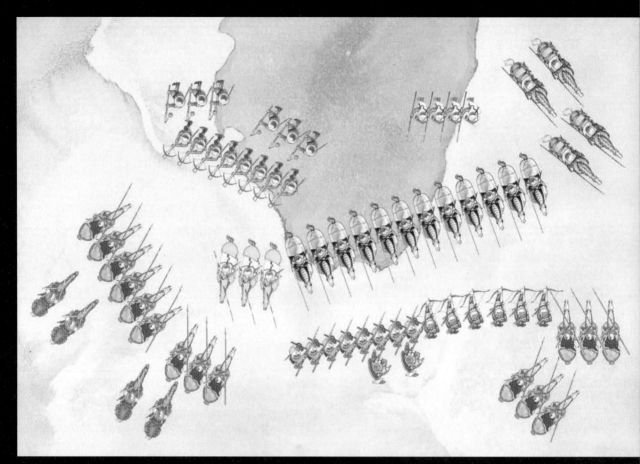

Top: DBA Online was a comprehensive digital version of the rules for cult tabletop wargame De Bellis Antiquitatis. It began Wargaming's long association with fans of military history.

Above and Left: Massive Assault took Wargaming's turn-based expertize and placed it in a mainstream sci-fi setting. It was a great success, spawning three sequels.

HISTORY OF THE GAME

Wargaming was born from Victor Kislyi's early love of (unsurprisingly) wargames. Like many children in Belarus he grew up with a strong love for both military history and chess. But after seeing the famous series of matches between Deep Blue and Garry Kasparov he became convinced that computers, not people, were the future of games. Kislyi's first game, before Wargaming as a company was even formed, was a play-by-email turn-based strategy called Iron Age that he created with his brother. As he once remarked glibly in an interview that it was played by four people – him, his brother and "two others". Eventually his brother and one of the other players stopped playing and Iron Age lost 50% of its playerbase.

Despite these humble origins Kislyi persevered. After spending time in America, he got involved with the historical miniatures community, inspiring him to create Wargaming and devise DBA Online, an adaptation of the miniatures game De Bellis Antiquitatis. The DBA playerbase was small, but the success of the online version meant that enormous amounts of them converted over to the digital game. Wargaming were encouraged, and pressed on to create Massive Assault, a series of sci-fi turn-based strategy games. They were critically and commercially successful, especially in Russia, but crucially they had entered the turn-based market at exactly the wrong time. Publishers were convinced turn-based strategy was a dead end, and with digital distribution not yet a viable alternative, Wargaming were forced to adapt. So they began work on Order of War, a real time strategy game set in World War II, and channelling their love of military history. It was a huge, authentic and historically accurate World War II experience, that helped them secure a publishing deal with Square Enix. Unfortunately, Wargaming were once again a victim of bad timing, releasing Order of War hot-on-the-heels of

Relic Entertainment's Company of Heroes, one of the most critically acclaimed World War II strategy games ever made. Company of Heroes had a strong, entrenched community of military enthusiasts, and Wargaming struggled to pry them free.

The company was stuck with a dilemma. Their favoured genre wasn't doing very well and boxed sales were trending down all over the world, but especially in their key market: Russia. What had been successful was an influx of free-to-play MMOs from China and Korea, so that's what they decided to make. For the first few months of World of Tanks' development it was a fantasy arena battle game. Then one day they came across a simple, free-to-play, isometric naval warfare sim called Navy Field. Wargaming realized they could play to their strengths, they knew little about fantasy MMOs, but years of historical wargaming and research for Order of War meant they knew a lot about tanks. They would fuse what they knew to the free-to-play model, and create something completely different from anything else on the market. Traditional gaming publishers were not as easily convinced, worried that the combination of an unusual idea, a determination to go free-to-play and a large market in the traditionally piracy-ridden Russia simply would not work, so Wargaming resolved to gamble everything and self-publish.

This time, Wargaming were determined to succeed. They learnt their mistakes from previous games. While Company of Heroes' loyal fanbase of military enthusiasts had thwarted Order of War's ambitions, that same community could be harnessed for World of Tanks. Instead of relying solely on traditional game advertising they deliberately targeted museums, military history enthusiasts and wargamers, basically anyone who loved tanks. It was a strategy honed in Russia but eventually copied by the West.

When I first heard of Wargaming they were sponsoring a tank show at the Tank Museum, Bovington, Dorset, who they've retained close ties with ever since. All these new gamers were invited to a lengthy, constantly updated a beta version where the game could be constantly tweaked and adapted to suit their gaming requirements.

The strategy was hugely successful. The number of players spiked and Wargaming found themselves frantically upgrading their server infrastructure to keep up with the unexpected demand. In 2011 World of Tanks set a Guinness World Record for the largest number of players on a single server, a record they've broken several times since. Currently the game has 110 million registered users. About 119,999,996 more than Iron Age!

Much of what we know today about World of Tanks was refined during that long Russia beta model. When the game first entered alpha, it contained only six tanks and one map. By the closed beta version, that number had grown to several dozen. Today it stands at over 300. This also explains why the Eastern front forces were the first to be fleshed out, with American tanks following just in time for the Western release. After a successful Western launch many more tanks would come, the U.S., Soviet and German factions were expanded, while the British, French, Chinese and Japanese armies also joined the game, as well as dozens of maps and various game modes.

Throughout the game's development Wargaming have continued to experiment. Early on the main "endgame" mode was Clan Wars, which hailed back to Wargaming's roots by using a turn-based strategy map to put battles in the context of a larger war over resources. While this appealed to players used to highly organised raids and MMO guild play, they didn't suit those who wanted decisive one-off battles or tournaments, especially e-sports enthusiasts. As a result, Wargaming began experimenting with other forms of high level competitive play, enjoying great success in e-sports circles as a result. A large part of that is Wargaming's continual push to create modes that reward the aggressive, entertaining play that e-sports audiences want to see, rather than tactically sensible but visually uninteresting sniper matches, like Tank Battle or Strongholds.

By 2011 Wargaming was a huge company, yet dedicated entirely to producing a single game. Rather than putting all their money into World of Tanks and risking player burnout, they began to develop World of Warplanes and World of Warships, based around air and naval warfare respectively. The theory was that if gamers ever became bored with tanks, they could easily switch to one of the other titles, rather than one created by a different company.

In 2014, World of Tanks saw a milestone they'd never considered possible five years previously. After years as a PC exclusive, the game was finally ported to the Xbox. The game that big publishers had once passed on for being too niche was now a bone fide mainstream hit.

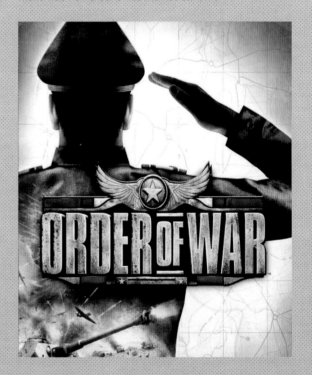

Above and Opposite: Order of War harnessed Wargaming's love of World War II. Without it, World of Tanks would not exist.

IN THE GARAGE

The garage is where you'll spend the majority of your non-battle time in World of Tanks. It houses all your tanks and allows you to re-equip them, research new parts, change crew, buy new tanks and more.

MENU – See page 54 for a full explanation of settings and what they mean.

PLATOON – A platoon is a small group of players that can join games together. Be careful not to platoon together if you are too many levels apart or the low level player will be dragged into high level battles.

REPAIR AND RELOAD – See page 36 for an explanation of repair costs and ammo types.

YOUR ACCOUNT

CURRENT TANK

VEHICLE STATS – See page 34 for a full breakdown of what these mean.

CHAT

YOUR TANKS

CHANGE TANK CAMOUFLAGE SKIN

NOTIFICATIONS – This will let you know the results of a match if you didn't watch it to the end, and what rewards you got.

FRIENDS LIST

DEPOT VIEW – Shows all the modules, equipment and consumables you currently have. This can be useful if you want to move them between tanks, or check that you haven't any equipment going unused.

MISSIONS – If you're familiar with MMO daily quests, this is a similar thing. You're given targets such as "Destroy 20 medium tanks" and are rewarded with XP, items or currency.

CREW – See page 42 for a full breakdown of crew skills and experience.

STORE VIEW – Allows you to directly purchase modules, equipment and consumables. This can also be done from other screens, but this offers an alternative.

SERVICE RECORD – Shows your career stats and achievements.

BATTLE – See page 50 for a breakdown of the different battle modes

CURRENCY – The three currencies are Gold, Credits and Experience. Go to page 46 for a full explanation of how they work.

UPGRADES – The components of your tank, gun, turret, engine, tracks, and radio. See page 38 for more on upgrades.

EQUIPMENT – Passive upgrade items, such as camouflage netting. Some can be moved between tanks freely, others cost money to remove and refit. See page 30 for a complete explanation.

CONSUMABLES – Similar to equipment, but must be activated to use and can only be used once. See page 32 for more on Consumables.

AMMUNITION

ON THE BATTLEFIELD

Once you are on the battlefield the screen changes, but all the information you need to battle effectively is visible. You must learn how to use the many tools at your disposal if you want to make the most of your time in action.

SCORE and TEAM LINEUPS – This shows the number and type of remaining tanks on both sides, as well as the total destroyed by each side.

RETICLE – The triangular arrow in the centre screen displays where your gun is currently targeted.

BATTLE CLOCK – Indicates how long you have left to battle.

TEAM PANEL – Ordered by tier. Destroyed vehicles fade from the lineup.

FRAME RATE AND PING/LAG INDICATOR

VEHICLE CONDITION – A diagram to show the status of your vehicle, its modules and crew.

VEHICLE MARKER – A customizable icon to show tier, name, hit points and more on both friendly and enemy vehicles.

AMMUNITION – Equipment and consumables are also displayed here if you have them.

MINIMAP – Your essential guide to what's happening on the battlefield.

ENEMY IN VIEW – If you have a line of sight to an enemy vehicle, shoot away! Note the line on the minimap.

TARGET ACQUIRED – See how the enemy tank is outlined in red when your central marker is on it. You can also see the damage taken and remaining HPs. Friendlies are marked in green.

SNIPER MODE – Your shots will be much more effective if you zoom in and aim carefully. Remember to allow the aiming to finish – the green circle will stop moving once you are locked on target.

SUCCESS! – Fire accurately and you should do damage. Maybe you'l destroy another tank. Note how the score has changed, and both vehicle lists are updated immediately.

VEHICLE DESTROYED – The battle is over for you. Observe how the Vehicle Condition display has changed. From this point you may follow surviving members of your team to see how the battle ends.

YOUR FIRST ROLL OUT

Here are my top tips for how to make your first battle, and the next few, a little more productive. They aren't high level tactical strategies, just tips that are immediately useful and easy to pick up.

1 Tier I tanks only have access to six maps. Two open farmland maps, two hill fights and two city fights. I'm using one of those maps, Himmelsdorf, as an illustration here.

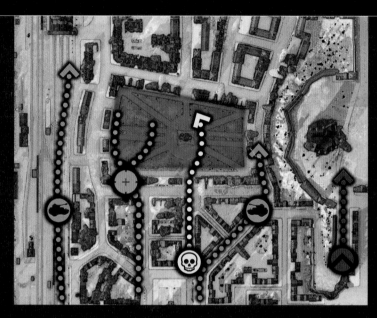

SNIPING – Most World of Tanks maps have a few good sniper spots that can be camped to try and catch onrushing tanks in unawares. This works fairly well in low-level matches as new players often charge recklessly forward, presenting you with an easy target. However, if both teams act cautiously matches can become a dull stalemate. If you find you enjoy sniping, consider investing in tank destroyers in future.

KAMIKAZE SCOUTING – A cheap tactic for quickly racking up experience on early maps, simply charge directly at the enemy, earning multiple spotter credits, and hope your team takes them out after your demise. It's a decent way to farm XP, but it won't help your team or make you any better at the game.

(ORANGE) ACTION STATIONS – One of the first lessons to learn is to avoid moving out into the open in the centre of the map. Tanks caught out here are vulnerable tanks. If you want to attack, make sure you are flanking or using cover.

FLANK & SPOT – There are many reasons to flank. Some flanking routes go all the way around behind the enemy to attack their control zone. Others will get you to a useful sniping perch half

way across the map. The important thing is to use cover to keep yourself hidden as you move. If you find you prefer spotting, continue along the light tank line.

TO HILL OR NOT TO HILL? – Himmelsdorf features a giant hill that offers a great viewpoint of the battlefield. The problem is it's so steep some tanks will take forever to climb it. Don't be seduced by easy sniping, only attempt the hill climb in fast tanks.

2 HUG THE CORNER

Using the corners of buildings as cover is vitally important. Try to show as little hull as possible to the enemy until your own turret is in view.

3 TRACKED

All tanks have locational damage with different effects. Some have exposed ammo racks, others have poorly armoured turrets, etc. The simplest and most universal trick shot you can learn though is to shoot for the tracks, which can briefly immobilise a tank, making it easy to finish off.

4 DON'T FEAR ARTILLERY (YET)

In your first few games you shouldn't have to worry about artillery at all. So feel free to hide behind walls and houses. In future you'll be forced to retreat if you feel you've been spotted, unless you want a shell dropped on your head.

5 SHORTCUTS

Remember, you are a tank! This means you can ram right through a lot of obstacles. If you are in a stalemate with an enemy, consider smashing through a wall to flank them.

6 TRY AGAIN

If your tank is destroyed it gets left on the battlefield until the match ends, but you don't have to stay! Instead you can go back to your garage and hop in a different tank to play again. You'll still get all the experience and rewards you would've if you'd stayed through the match.

7 LEARN THE KEYS

Here are some useful several useful keyboard shortcuts to learn:

Left Shift – Sniper view
Right click on target – Lock aim
Hold down right mouse – Move view without moving turret
Space – Instant stop
Double tap R – Full speed ahead
Double tap F – Full speed reverse

8 WOLFPACK TACTICS

Don't head off alone if you can avoid it, instead pay attention to where your teammates are heading and try and form a group of three or four tanks. This is known as a "wolfpack", by moving together, attacking aggressively and ganging up on stray tanks you become far more effective than you would as individuals. If you enjoy Wolfpacking then consider investing in medium tanks in future.

EQUIPMENT

Equipment is a type of item that is added to your tank in one of the three equipment slots. It provides a passive bonus to tank performance. Unlike consumables, equipment does not need to be activated by the player and can be used an infinite number of times.

There are two types of equipment: REMOVABLE EQUIPMENT can be equipped or removed at no cost, and can be mounted on all vehicles. COMPLEX EQUIPMENT can only be removed in one of three ways.
• Pay 10 Gold to demount the equipment and return it to your depot (where it can be mounted on another tank).
• Destroy the equipment, freeing the slot but losing the equipment.
• Sell the tank with the equipment mounted, which will net you half the cost of the equipment back.
   Some complex equipment will only work on specific vehicles.

REMOVABLE EQUIPMENT

 CAMOUFLAGE NET – Produces a bonus to camouflage when a tank is stationary for more than three seconds. The bonus is 10% for light and medium tanks, 5% for heavy tanks and artillery and 15% for tank destroyers. This is an excellent piece of equipment for tank destroyers, particularly those who favour sniping or ambush, such as the Hetzer and StuG. It also works very well on turreted tank destroyers like the M10 Wolverine and M18 Hellcat, as rotating the turret does not count as 'moving' for the purposes of breaking camouflage. The camouflage net is the cheapest piece of removable equipment and if you plan to use tank destroyers at all I recommend buying one.

 BINOCULAR TELESCOPE – Gives a 25% bonus to view range for tanks that are stationary for more than three seconds. Much like the camouflage net, this works very well on tank destroyers, who are typically stationary for long periods while they wait

in ambush. However, it can also work well on other "sniper" tanks such as the E50 and Panther.

 TOOLBOX – Give a 25% increase to your crew repair speed, enabling them to rapidly repair broken modules. The main use of the toolbox is to rapidly repair broken tracks, as a tank with broken tracks is rendered stationary and exposed. The toolbox is useful on just about any tank, but especially those with inexperienced crew who have yet to level up their own repair skills. Veterans will often strap a toolbox onto a new tank for its first few battles to give them an edge while they earn upgrades.

COMPLEX EQUIPMENT

 RAMMER – Reduces loading time by 10%, and as such is highly recommended for tanks that enjoy inflicting heavy-duty damage. The rammer comes in four varieties: medium tank/tank destroyer, large tank/tank destroyer, medium artillery and large artillery. In general, rammer size is dictated by gun size, rather than tank size. Usually, tanks with guns under 105mm use the medium rammer, while those with guns over 105mm use the large one (for artillery the threshold is 155mm). As always check before you buy. Rammers cannot be fitted to any gun that uses an autoloader.

 COATED OPTICS – Very similar to binoculars, coated optics provide a 10% view distance bonus. However, this bonus is active at all times, not just when stationary, as the Binocular Telescope. As such this works better than binoculars if you are driving highly mobile and aggressive tanks, especially scouts. This piece of Complex Equipment is available as an upgrade for most tanks.

IMPROVED VENTILATION – Adds 5% to all crew skills, making it one of the most universally useful pieces of equipment available. Boosting crew skills improves view range, aim time, accuracy, turret move rate, radio range and many more. Even if you get your crew to 100% skills, this will boost them to 105%. Ventilation comes in three versions, Class One covers all light tanks (and the British Vickers Medium Mk I), Class Two covers medium tanks (except the Vickers) and Class Three covers heavy tanks. Tank destroyers and artillery are split between them. "Open" vehicles, i.e. Hummell are not able to make use of Improved Ventilation.

"WET" AMMO RACK – Encases the ammo rack in water held in plastic. Thus when the ammo rack is hit the water is released, instantly dousing any fire. In practice this adds 50% to the health of your ammo rack. The primary use of this is on tanks that have exposed or poorly placed ammo racks that are prone to getting shot, such as the British Crusader and Soviet T-44, to increase the durability of the tank.

FILL TANKS WITH CO_2 – A similar trick to the ammo rack, only this time with the fuel tanks, granting them 50% durability. Again this is best used on tanks that specifically have a problem with exposed fuel tanks, such as the T-43. This upgrade is available on vehicles of most nations.

CYCLONE FILTER – A 50% hitpoint boost, just like CO_2 tanks, but for the engine. Similarly, they can only be used on Soviet and Chinese tanks. Note that this does not counteract damage from the "Remove Speed Governor" consumable, which is calculated as percentage of engine hitpoints. This is only available for Russian or Chinese vehicles.

ENHANCED SUSPENSION – There are a huge number of different kinds of suspension, but all of them have the same effect: +10 weight limit, +20% suspension hit points, and a 50% reduction in fall damage. The only difference is which tanks they can be fitted to. While the weight limit improvement here can be useful to allow you to carry more upgrades, the main draw is the increased suspension hit points, which helps prevent your tank from being 'tracked' (i.e: shot in the tracks in such a way as to briefly immobilize it). A tank that is tracked out in the open is usually a dead tank, so these are a good investment. Just make sure you check which tanks each type of suspension is compatible with before buying.

SPALL LINER – Improves protection from explosions, ramming and injury to crew. It comes in four varieties: light, medium, heavy and superheavy, depending on the weight of your tank (be sure to check before buying). The equations that govern damage are very complicated, but the quick version is that this works best on heavy tanks and heavily armoured tank destroyers such as the British AT7. For obvious reasons it also works well on good ramming tanks, such as the KV-5.

ENHANCED GUN LAYING DRIVE – Reduces aiming time by 10%. There is some debate over whether this or the vertical stabiliser is more useful. Generally speaking the gun laying drive is best used on tanks that intend to remain stationary, such as Tank Destroyers and Artillery. Some of these may also wish to purchase a vertical stabiliser, allowing them to enjoy both bonuses at once.

VERTICAL STABILIZER – Reduces aiming penalties by 20%, but does not improve aim overall. In laymans terms this means that your targeting reticule will start off 20% smaller, but once it has finished aiming it will be the same size as before. In a practical sense this will generally improve aim time (similar to an enhanced gun laying drive) and make your tank more accurate on the move. As such the vertical stabilizer is more popular with light, medium and heavy tanks than the enhanced gun laying drive, though some may wish to combine both to double effect. The MK I stabiliser is for light and medium tanks, the MK II is for heavy tanks.

ADDITIONAL GROUSERS – Improve your tanks ability to handle rough terrain by a small amount. Note that on very light tanks this may offer little benefit, as the bonuses granted by the grousers will be largely cancelled out by the additional weight of equipping them.

CONSUMABLES

Consumables work like equipment, but instead of working every time they are destroyed (or "consumed") upon first use. Some consumables offer passive performance bonuses such as equipment, and are consumed as soon as you start a match equipped with one. Others have to be manually activated using the 4–6 keys and are generally used to repair your tank or heal your crew. Pay attention to which is which – you don't want to use up your precious chocolate by mistake.

There are two broad types of consumables. Originally REGULAR CONSUMABLES were bought with credits and PREMIUM CONSUMABLES were bought with gold, but as of patch 8.5 premium consumables can now be bought with credits as well, they just cost significantly more (four times as much as the most expensive regular consumable).

REGULAR CONSUMABLES

SMALL REPAIR KIT
3,000 credits

Repairs one chosen damaged module when activated. Both tracks count as a single module for the purposes of repair. The primary use of this consumable is to carry out emergency repairs to the tracks if your tank is caught out in the open. This won't affect your repair costs at the end of the match, it will just keep you functioning until the end of the match.

SMALL FIRST AID KIT
3,000 credits

Heals one chosen injured crew member when activated in much the same way as the repair kit. Used to keep your crew in good health, as injured crew members impose severe penalties on a tank. If the entire crew is injured your tank counts as being destroyed.

MANUAL FIRE EXTINGUISHERS
3,000 credits

Activating this consumable immediately stops your tank from being on fire. Fire causes continual damage to a tank the longer it goes on for, so speed is of the essence when activating this consumable. The faster you click the less damage you will take.

100-OCTANE GASOLINE
5,000 credits

Increases engine power (and thus acceleration) and turret movement speed for 5% for one match. This consumable is only available for American, British, German and French vehicles, and only when they are equipped with gasoline engines (rather than diesel). This consumable doesn't require activation, it is automatically used when you start a match with it equipped.

LEND-LEASE OIL
5,000 credits

Increases engine power by 5% in exactly the same way as 100-octane Gasoline, but works on any engine and is only available to Soviet vehicles. There is an identical version available for Chinese and Japanese vehicles called Quality Oil. As before, this consumable does not need to be activated, it automatically fires up when you start a match with it equipped.

REMOVED SPEED GOVERNOR

3,000 credits

A special consumable that is never actually "consumed". Activating it just turns it on or off. When activated a vehicle receives a 10% bonus to engine power, but causes damage to its engine when accelerating. This bonus stacks with Lend-Lease Oil via multiplication, resulting in a 15.5% total bonus. This consumable is only available for Soviet and Chinese vehicles.

PREMIUM CONSUMABLES

LARGE REPAIR KIT

50 gold or 20,000 credits

Adds a passive 10% bonus crew repair speed when equipped. When activated it works just like a small repair kit, only it repairs all currently damaged modules instead of just one. The bonus is lost once the kit is used.

LARGE FIRST AID KIT

50 gold or 20,000 credits

Adds 15% resistance to crew injury while equipped. When employed it works similiar to it's smaller cousin, only it heals all currently injured crew members instead of just one. The passive bonus is lost once the kit is used.

AUTOMATIC FIRE EXTINGUISHERS

50 gold or 20,000 credits

Works exactly like the manual fire extinguisher only it activates automatically half a second after a fire starts. It also provides a passive bonus reducing your chance to catch fire by 10%. The passive bonus is lost once the extinguisher is used.

105-OCTANE GASOLINE

50 gold or 20,000 credits

Increases engine power in exactly the same way as 100-octane Gasoline, only it provides a 10% bonus instead of 5%. As before there is no activation for this item, it is used the moment you enter battle with it equipped.

EXTRA COMBAT RATIONS

- Case of Cola
- Chocolate
- Pudding and Tea
- Strong Coffee
- Improved Combat Rations

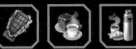

ONIGIRI

50 gold or 20,000 credits

All of these consumables work exactly the same way. Each adds a flat 10% to all crew skills for the entire match. Crew perks are also improved. This bonus still works on crew members who have 100% in all their skills, taking them up to 110%, or even more when combined with other bonuses like Improved Ventilation. There is no activation for this item, it is activated the moment you enter battle with it equipped.

Each nation has their own version of rations. Soviet vehicles get Extra Combat Rations, Chinese Vehicles get Improved Combat Rations, American Vehicles get a Case of Cola, Japanese vehicles get Onigiri, French Vehicles get Strong Coffee, German vehicles get Chocolate and British Vehicles get Pudding and Tea. The latter is a reference to the fact that British Tanks are always equipped with a Boiling Vessel (or BV), so that the crew can enjoy their tea without having to venture outside the tank. As you know, the British are very serious about their tea!

STATISTICS

Before we start, a word of warning: all statistics are relative. The skills as they are displayed in the Garage assume that your crew all have a skill of 100%. Of course, you will almost never have a screw with exactly 100% skill (not least because the commander provides a bonus to other crewmembers). You may have less or you may have more, so take the statistics you see on the Garage screen as relative, not absolute.

HIT POINTS

If you've played a video game before chances are you're familiar with the concept of hit points. They dictate how often you can get damaged before you are killed. Hitpoints are not the same as a tank's armour. It is possible to have poor armour and good hitpoints, which means you are damaged by almost every shot but can take that damage for a long time. Conversely, a tank with good armour and poor hitpoints will see most shots ineffectually bounce off, but any that get through will destroy it quickly.

WEIGHT/LOAD LIMIT

This is expressed as xx/yy where x is how much your tank currently weighs and y is how much weight your suspension can support. Obviously if you reach the limit, you'll be unable to add extra equipment or modules to your tank until you research better suspension!

ENGINE POWER

Better engine power means more speed, better acceleration and a host of other benefits. It is usually opposed by weight, so the heavier your tank the more power you'll need to maintain performance. Several consumables can boost engine power including gasoline, oil and removed speed governor.

TOP SPEED

How fast the tank goes. This is calculated from your engine power and weight – the more power you have, the faster you go, the more weight you have, the slower you go. Don't expect to cruise at your top speed all the time, some tanks will only reach it when they have a long flat stretch of ground. Alternatively, you might go even faster if you're going downhill.

TRAVERSE SPEED

How fast your can turn. A tank with a high top speed but a poor traverse speed will struggle to make tight turns and end up lapping the battlefield in big, broad circles. You can improve your traverse speed by improving your engine or suspension. Confusingly, any improvements from a better engine won't be shown on the garage screen, but the suspension will.

HULL ARMOUR

Armour is expressed as $xx/yy/zz$. Where x is the front armour, y is the side armour and z is the rear armour. The number represents the thickness of your armour, so larger numbers are better. However, this doesn't tell the whole story as the shape of the armour also factors heavily into how well it withstands fire. The angle of the armour matters a lot, which is why you'll see "sloped armour" mentioned a lot in this book. Put simply, it is harder to penetrate armour at an angle than head on, so sloped armour can often be stronger than it appears. An alternative to sloped armour is spaced armour, which consists of thin armour plates with a gap in between them. Most shells tend to deform or disintegrate when they hit the first plate, leading them to lack momentum and penetration by the time they reach the second. Spaced armour is particularly effective against HEAT rounds, which often explode harmlessly at the first plate.

TURRET ARMOUR

Exactly the same as hull armour, but for your turret. Tanks whose turret armour is better than their hull armour benefit from going hull down (using terrain to expose only your turret). Unlike hull armour, it is possible to improve a tank's turret armour by researching better turrets.

STANDARD SHELL DAMAGE

The damage you do when your shell hits and penetrates. It is expressed as a range because a whole host of factors can influence shell damage, making it very unpredictable.

STANDARD SHELL PENETRATION

How much armour a shell will usually penetrate. It's expressed as a range due to the unpredictable nature of penetration. Note that this doesn't mean that you'll definitely penetrate armour of the thickness indicated, as sloping/spaced armour has an effect on penetration.

RATE OF FIRE

How fast your gun can fire. This statistic might be a little deceptive in the case of autoloaders, which can fire several shots extremely quickly, but then require a long time to reload before they can fire again.

TURRET TRAVERSE SPEED

Put simply, this is how fast you can turn your turret. A high traverse speed is desirable to help track fast moving targets, and thus is vital to anti-scout tactics. A slow moving turret puts you at a disadvantage if an enemy can circle around you faster than you can turn to face them.

VIEW RANGE

The range at which you can see other tanks. The higher it is, the further away you will spot them. View Range is particularly useful for scouts and snipers. Note that while this stat does factor in things such as commander skills, it won't include situational bonuses like the binocular

telescope equipment, which only works when the vehicle is stationary.

SIGNAL RANGE

The range at which you can report the location of other tanks to allies. Any friendly tank inside your radio range will see the tanks you have spotted on their map. They will in turn relay those locations to every tank within their radio range. Thus maintaining a strong chain of radio links all the way from the forward scouts to the rear artillery is vitally important to an effective team. Radio range is most important to scouts, who are likely to venture ahead of the main formation.

HIDDEN STATISTICS

Not every statistic is displayed on the front of the Garage page. Here are a few of the other calculations working behind the scenes.

CAMOUFLAGE

Dictates how likely you are to be spotted by enemy tanks. It can be increased by skins and the camouflage net equipment. Camouflage is especially important to scouts and tank destroyers. Camouflage is halved when the tank is moving, unless you're in a light tank.

TERRAIN RESISTANCE

Expresses how well a tank can deal with various types of rough terrain, can be improved by using the additional grousers equipment. Weight is a factor in calculating this statistic, loading your tank up with too much stuff will make it struggle on rough terrain.

SHELL SPEED

How fast the tank's round flies through the air, this has an effect on armour penetration (at least for AP rounds). APCR ammo is generally faster than AP ammo. Rounds will slow down the further they fly, making penetration worse at long distances. Slower shells will also fire in more of an arc through the air.

REPAIR AND RELOAD

One thing you'll quickly learn in World of Tanks is that your wounds aren't magically healed between battles. While your crew may jury rig broken tracks during a match, when you finish you'll have to deal with that damage, as well as take stock of any ammunition you've expended.

Repairing and reloading is done from the garage screen. Simply click on the Service tab and you'll be presented with a series of options relating to your tank's health and what kind of shells you're packing. This is what it all means:

REPAIR

This is the big health bar at the top of the Service screen. Repair costs aren't a factor at low levels, but they gradually increase the higher the tier of tank you're driving, eventually becoming a significant drain on resources.

Tanks can be set to repair and reload ammo automatically. This is extremely useful at low tiers, but best avoided at higher levels when the exobitant cost of repairs can suddenly bankrupt a player.

Premium tanks typically have much lower repair costs than their same tier counterparts. This means that buying a good premium tank in order to farm credits to keep your other tanks in top fighting condition can be a very good idea. Many high level players will maintain a Tier VIII premium tank, such as a Löwe, purely to make money.

RELOADING

The service tab is also used to load, reload and change ammunition for your tanks. Similiar to repairing, this gets steadily more expensive the higher the level of tank you're using, becoming a significant factor at high levels. As with repairs, premium tanks are much cheaper to reload.

TYPES OF AMMUNITION

Ammo is divided into standard ammo and premium ammo. Standard ammo is purchased for a small amount of credits, while premium ammo can be purchased with gold or a larger amount of credits, much like consumables. Tanks carry three different types of ammo into battle and you can switch between them by pressing the 1-3 keys. Switching ammo is not instant, it requires you to do a full reload, which may leave you vulnerable if you are in the middle of a fight.

STANDARD AMMO
ARMOUR PIERCING (AP)

 Armour Piercing ammo is designed to punch through armour in order to damage the inner workings of a tank. AP ammo penetrates armour better the faster it moves, which makes it more effective the closer you are to your target. In a practical sense AP ammo will do good damage if it penetrates, but none at all if it fails to penetrate. AP is the standard ammo for most tanks and tank destroyers in the game, if you're unsure what to use, go with AP. AP sometimes appears as a premium ammo type for artillery, where it should be used with caution, as the lack of splash damage makes it hard to aim.

HIGH EXPLOSIVE (HE)

High Explosive rounds do not attempt to penetrate armour, instead they explode on impact, causing massive damage to poorly armoured tanks and overcoming some armour by dint of sheer explosive force. On the battlefield this translates as a round that can do some damage even if it doesn't penetrate armour, and does a lot if a very large shell is used. HE rounds are the primary ammo for artillery, but they are also useful on any tank equipping a low velocity, high-calibre howitzer. Other tanks may want to switch to HE when attacking lightly armoured targets, such as artillery, or when defending a capture point, as inflicting even a small amount of damage will reset the capture timer.

PREMIUM AMMO
ARMOUR PIERCING COMPOSITE RIGID (APCR)

Armour Piercing Composite Rigid rounds comprise of a strong armour piercing core surrounded by a lightweight casing. This essentially makes them souped up AP rounds that cost more to equip. APCR rounds move faster through the air than AP rounds, which means they penetrate better, but you may have to adjust your aim when using them. They are slightly worse at dealing with sloped armour and long range compared to AP ammo, but this usually isn't enough to overcome their superior default penetration. Use APCR ammo when AP ammo struggles to penetrate – if you can afford it.

PREMIUM HIGH EXPLOSIVE (HE)

Premium High Explosive rounds are a more expensive version of regular HE rounds that usually come with some sort of bonus, like a higher splash

radius. They fill the function of premium ammunition or some artillery.

HIGH EXPLOSIVE ANTI-TANK (HEAT)

High Explosive Anti-Tank rounds are not merely one of the military's best acronyms, but also an effective tool. A HEAT round uses a shaped charge to penetrate armour instead of speed, meaning it fires like a HE round, but penetrates like AP. It has extremely high armour penetration that is not dependant on muzzle velocity, making it great for howitzers, however it does not deal with sloped armour anywhere near as well as the AP ammo types. For complicated reasons it is not advisable to fire HEAT ammo at tracks, as it will often prematurely detonate on the outer armour without reaching the tracks. Most artillery can use HEAT rounds, but it should be used with caution as it does not have any splash damage and artillery are notorious inaccurate.

HIGH EXPLOSIVE SQUASH HEAD (HESH)

High Explosive Squash Head rounds spread a "paste" of explosives on the surface they are fired at, which then detonates. This does not penetrate armour but instead causes a concussive blast throughout the tank, damaging internal equipment and injuring crew. This unusual behaviour translates into a HE shell with far better penetration values, making it a straight upgrade for HE users who can afford them.

UPGRADES

AMERICAN T1 CUNNINGHAM

FIRST UPGRADES: Congratulations! You have the fastest Tier I tank in the game! These qualities can be enhanced further by researching the Cunningham V8 engine. Once that's done you'll be looking to invest in the Cunningham's semi-automatic guns, which work like autoloaders, letting you fire five fast shots before a long reload. This turns you into a hit-and-run glass cannon. The main debate will be between the 37mm Browning Semiautomatic Gun, which hits harder, and the 20mm Hispano-Suiza Birkigt Gun, which fires faster.

PLANNING AHEAD: The M2 light opens up the American light tank tree whose tanks hit hard, but are often large and conspicuous. Meanwhile, the T18 introduces you to the American tank destroyers. There are two lines, both are mobile and hard-hitting but one has turrets and one does not. I suggest heading for the M18 Hellcat for the highly entertaining turret-based line. Also, the T2 medium tank leads to both U.S. Mediums, which are versatile support tanks good at firing on the move, and the Heavy Tank line, which features heavily armoured turrets and good gun depression, allowing them to go hull down. Finally, American artillery is known for its destructive firepower and huge splash damage.

SOVIET MS-1

FIRST UPGRADES: A stock MS-1 is slower and weaker than its U.S. and German counterparts but boasts strong front armour. At the beginning, you'll want to focus on upgrading your gun. The 37mm B-3 is a decent upgrade, but what you're really looking for is the 45mm mod. 1932. This is the best single shot gun available to starter tanks. It's slow to aim and relatively inaccurate, but packs a huge punch. This is a theme you'll need to get used to if you plan to stick with Russian tanks.

PLANNING AHEAD: By grabbing your gun you'll be opening the door to the AT-1 Tank Destroyer. Soviet tank destroyers generally have poor armour, but high camouflage, making them ideal for ambush tactics. If you're interested in Soviet Heavy Tanks, which are excellent toe-to-toe brawlers with powerful but inaccurate guns, then you'll need to unlock the T-26. All other light tanks eventually lead to the mighty T-34 and the Jack-of-All-Trades Soviet medium line, which is recommended for beginners. Finally, picking up the upgraded tracks will open up the SU-18, leading to Soviet artillery, which features good accuracy and a high arc of fire, making them ideal for hitting tanks hiding deceptively behind buildings and bridges.

GERMAN LIECHTRAKTOR

FIRST UPGRADES: Unlike the MS-1 you'll find your stock gun is actually rather good, and there's a strong case for sticking with it throughout your stay in Tier I, although the 2cm Breda offers an a autocannon at the expense of accuracy. Instead, focus on upgrading your terrible engine, giving yourself a massive speed boost. Points will also be well spent in upgrading your turret, giving you a huge view range advantage over your fellow starter tanks.

PLANNING AHEAD: The German light tank line is extremely well rounded and highly recommend if you're interested in scouting. German medium tanks tend to be snipers with highly accurate long range guns. German tank destroyers offer two lines, one of which starts with traditional ambush tanks like the Hetzer and StuG III and ends up with heavily armoured behemoths. The other, which features the various Waffenträgers, consists entirely of increasingly powerful glass cannons. The German heavy tank line evolves much as they did in World War II, with increasingly ludicrous superheavy tanks introduced, which are thankfully more useful in the game than in war. Finally, German artillery places a premium on accuracy and mobility.

BRITISH VICKERS MEDIUM MK I

FIRST UPGRADES: The Brits are the only faction to start the game with a medium tank, rather than a light tank. Unfortunately this turns out to be more of a curse than a blessing as the Vickers' large size is not made up for with strong armour. What it does have is three fantastic guns: The starting OQF 3-pounder Mk I is highly accurate but slow to aim, the fast firing 15mm Machine Gun BESA will shred all but the most heavily armoured low tier tanks and the QF 6-pounder 8 cwt Mk II packs a massive, if inaccurate, punch. Personally, I recommend the starter gun, as sniper tactics suit the Vickers. However, if you want the QF 6-pounder you'll need to upgrade your turret and suspension to mount it. It's also worth noting that many British tanks re-use the same radio, so grab one early and keep hold of it.

PLANNING AHEAD: British tanks are strange. The star attraction here is their light tank line, starting with the Cruiser III, which play more like small medium tanks than dedicated scouts only to mutate into the powerful Centurion medium tanks at high tiers. For now, the Cruiser I leads to a group of strangely slow and well-armoured light and medium tanks before giving way to heavy support tanks. Tank destroyers start fast and vulnerable and become slow but heavily armoured, artillery features short range but good firing arcs. Finally, there's a line of refitted American tanks, including the impressive Sherman Firefly.

FRENCH RENAULT FT

FIRST UPGRADES: The first thing you're going to want to do is upgrade your underpowered engine to get some more speed. After that you'll want to do something about your terrible starting gun. What you want is the Canon Raccourci Mle. 1934, which is accurate and fast firing. You'll need to upgrade your turret to mount it, but that's fine because the Renault is all about having a well armoured turret. After that you can dogfight to your heart's content, just don't stray too long range or your gun will lose all penetration.

PLANNING AHEAD: The French tech tree is a little odd in that instead of a traditional light/medium/heavy split it has two lines. The Hotchkiss H35 starts a long line of light tanks that eventually turn medium. Both work much the same way, starting out slow and heavily armoured before eventually becoming high speed glass cannons using their powerful autoloaders to fire several shots in one quick burst. French tank destroyers have solid guns but their armour is full of vulnerable weak spots, while their artillery are designed to move and fire quickly and accurately, even though this means they lack punch.

CHINESE RENAULT NC-31

FIRST UPGRADES: The Renault NC-31 behaves a lot better than the Renault FT, so the first thing you'll want to do is grab an engine upgrade. After that, get hold of the dependable 13.2mm Hotchkiss Mle. 1930, which will serve as a main gun for most of your career. After that you can upgrade whatever you want or just power through to the next tank.

PLANNING AHEAD: China is a fairly underdeveloped faction right now, so there's only one path to go down until Tier VI, which features a slew of tanks bought from other nations. From there, the 59-16 leads to a line of British-like light tanks that play like small medium tanks. At the same time, their heavy and medium tanks play much like their Soviet equivalents, which is no bad thing. There are currently no Chinese tank destroyers or artillery in the game.

JAPANESE RENAULT OTSU

FIRST UPGRADES: The Otsu is another Renault FT variant, and that means upgrading the engine early on before hunting for a better gun. Research the 37mm Infantry Gun Type 11 but don't equip it, instead make a beeline for the far superior 37mm Sogekihei. The 13mm Autocannon Type Ho is also an option, it just all depends if you want a big boom gun or a fast firing, low penetration autoloader.

PLANNING AHEAD: Japan is the newest faction in World of Tanks and thus has the least developed tech tree. At this stage you'll be asked to make a choice between their light tanks, which are agile and lightly armoured but with decent firepower and medium tanks, which are more cumbersome but have much more impressive weaponry. After that the lines reunite into a set of medium support tanks with substandard armour but good accuracy and firepower.

CREW

Although they may not initially seem like it your crew are one of the most important parts of your vehicle. Crew skills deliver an enormous number of passive bonuses to all aspects of your tank. This means a tank with a fully trained crew has a considerable advantage over a group of rookies.

You shouldn't generally concern yourself with crew skill for the first three tiers, as crew skills do not carry over between vehicles unless you retrain your crew but you'll be switching between tanks too quickly to make that worthwhile. But around Tiers IV and V crew training starts to become a serious advantage, and you should consider investing more in it.

CREW TRAINING

When getting new crew or retraining existing crew, there are three choices:

RAPID TRAINING COURSES – FREE
This is the basic form of crew training. Buying your crew directly from Rapid Training results in crew with 50% experience. Alternatively, you can use it to retrain existing crew, which will give them 80% of their original skill in a new vehicle of the same class (Heavy, Light, Medium, SPG or Tank Destroyer) or 60% of their original skill in a vehicle of a new class. You'll mostly use rapid training during the early tiers.

REGIMENTAL SCHOOL – 20,000 CREDITS
This upgraded school creates new crew members with 75% crew skill, or retrains them to 90% of their original skill (same class) or 80% (different class). This becomes more useful when you are using mid-tier tanks. The price is for the whole crew, however many crew members that may be.

TANK ACADEMY – 200 GOLD
Creates a new tank crew with 100% skill in their role or retrains them to 100% skill on a new tank. Very expensive and only worth considering at high levels.

EARNING EXPERIENCE

You can also improve your crew skills by earning experience through play. This works especially well if you have fully researched a tank (or bought a premium tank) as you can tick a checkbox to convert all additional experience (which would normally be wasted) into more crew experience. Completing personal missions rewards you with several premium tanks, excellent for training new crew members.

THE CREW SKILLS

Note that different vehicles will have different crew configurations. For example, a small tank may not have a loader, with those duties falling to the gunner instead. Conversely, a large tank may even have two loaders, or any one of many combinations.

MAIN ROLE

COMMANDER – A commander's proficiency affects the vehicle's view range. The higher their skill, the higher the view range. In addition, the commander also increases the skills of the rest of the crew a small amount in a similar fashion to chocolate or improved ventilation.

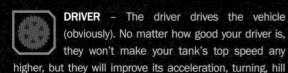 GUNNER – A gunner affects the vehicles aim time, accuracy and turret traverse rate. While they won't make your gun fire any faster, they'll make it aim faster, aim better and move quicker. If your gunner is knocked out you will take penalties to all these stats.

DRIVER – The driver drives the vehicle (obviously). No matter how good your driver is, they won't make your tank's top speed any higher, but they will improve its acceleration, turning, hill climbing and ability to handle rough terrain.

RADIO OPERATOR – The radio operator affects your vehicles radio range, which is the radius within which you can inform your fellow team members of enemy tank locations. Spotting enemies like this is a good way to earn experience. Losing your radio operator will reduce or completely remove your ability to do this.

LOADER – The loader loads the shells into the tank's gun. The better your loader, the better your reload time. If your loader is knocked out expect to see long reload times.

SKILLS AND PERKS

Once a crew member reaches 100% in their main role they begin to train a crew skill. Once they reach 100% in that they start again. A crew member can have multiple crew skills, but each new skill takes more and more experience to learn.

There are two types of crew skills, skills and perks. Skills work just like your main role, the bonus you get increases the higher the skill gets. Perks give a strong bonus when they reach 100% trained, but nothing until then.
Different skills and perks are available to different roles:

ALL ROLES

 REPAIR SKILL – Increases the speed at which the crew make emergency repairs to modules in much the same way as the toolbox equipment. Extremely useful on heavy and medium tanks, less useful on vulnerable tanks that are likely to be destroyed in one or two shots.

 FIREFIGHTING SKILL – Works much like repair, but for putting out fires instead. Fires are rarer than damaged modules, so unless you're using a vehicle prone to fires then you're usually better off with repair.

 CAMOUFLAGE SKILL – Increases your camouflage skill in a similar fashion to the camouflage net equipment. This is best used on tank destroyers and other snipers, along with light tanks, who use it to remain hidden while scouting.

 BROTHERS IN ARMS PERK – Once earned this perk gives a flat 5% bonuses to all crew abilities in much the same way as the improved ventilation equipment, which it also stacks with. This perk only works if every member of the tank has Brothers in Arms fully trained, otherwise it is useless.

SISTERHOOD OF STEEL PERK – This is exactly the same as Brothers in Arms, but for female crew members. The two perks are not compatible. If some crew members have Brothers in Arms and others have Sisterhood of Steel you will not get the bonus, all crew must have either one or the other.

COMMANDER

SIXTH SENSE PERK – Causes a red light bulb to appear in the middle of the HUD approximately three seconds after your vehicle has been spotted. It does not indicate if you have been unspotted, only when you go from hidden to visible. This is not particularly useful on heavy tanks which are not usually quick enough to react to being spotted.

MENTOR – The higher the mentor skill, the faster the other, non-commander crew members earn experience.

EAGLE EYE PERK – Highlights damaged modules on enemy tanks allowing you to exploit them. It only works on tanks you have spotted, not those spotted by your allies, and so is not very useful to long range snipers. Instead, it is best used on close range brawlers, or on scouts in a well co-ordinated team.

RECON SKILL – Increases the view range of a vehicle by a very small amount, but also helps the vehicle maintain its view range better when damaged. The latter effect is the more useful of the two, making this worthwhile on tough tanks that are likely to fight on after being damaged.

JACK OF ALL TRADES SKILL – This skill allows the commander to replace crew members who have been knocked out. While even with a high Jack of All Trades skill the commander will not be as good as the original crew member, they will be a lot better than nothing.

GUNNER

ARMOURER SKILL – Decreases the accuracy penalty for having a damaged gun. Like other, similar skills this is more useful on tanks that can take a beating than those that are typically destroyed immediately.

DEADEYE PERK – Increases the chance of a critical hit by 3% when fully trained. Has no effect with High Explosive ammunition and so should not be used on tanks likely to fire HE.

SNAP SHOT SKILL – Improves accuracy when rotating the turret. This effect stacks with the vertical stabilizer equipment.

DESIGNATED TARGET PERK – Makes enemies that are near your targeting reticule visible for two more seconds when detected, stopping them from slipping back into hidden status.

DRIVER

CLUTCH BRAKING SKILL – Increases a vehicles turn rate. Stacks with the additional grousers equipment and all the engine boosting consumables.

SMOOTH RIDE SKILL – Improves the vehicles accuracy during movement in a similar fashion to the snap shot skill with turret movement. Stacks with the vertical stabilizer equipment.

OFF ROAD DRIVING SKILL – Improves your vehicles ability to handle tricky terrain. Works in a similar fashion to the additional grousers equipment, which it stacks with.

CONTROLLED IMPACT SKILL – Reduces ramming damage taken by your vehicle and increases ramming damage done to enemies. Combine with a spall liner for a dedicated ramming tank.

 PREVENTATIVE MAINTENANCE PERK – Reduces the chance of fire in the engine. Stacks with the passive effect of the automatic fire extinguishers consumable.

RADIO OPERATOR

 SIGNAL BOOSTING SKILL – Increases radio range by up to 20% when fully trained. Useful on scout tanks.

 SITUATIONAL AWARENESS SKILL – Increases view range by up to 3% when fully trained. Stacks with the recon skill. This skill also boosts the sight range of allied tanks in your radio range.

 RELAYING SKILL – Boosts the radio range of allied tanks that are in your radio range.

 CALL FOR VENGEANCE PERK – If your tank is destroyed and your radio operator was not knocked out, you continue to report enemy positions for an additional two seconds, which can result in a nasty surprise for whoever killed you if artillery chooses to target your position.

LOADER

 SAFE STOWAGE PERK – Reduces the chance of your ammo rack exploding. Useful on tanks that have vulnerable ammo racks such as the British Crusader or Soviet T-44.

 ADRENALINE RUSH PERK – Reduces the reload time of your vehicle if it is damaged to below 10% health. For obvious reasons this works best on tanks with large hit point totals.

INTUITION PERK – Gives the loader a 17% chance to instantly switch shell type with no delay. Best used on tanks that find themselves switching between shells a lot.

SISTERHOOD OF STEEL

In 2015 World of Tanks introduced female crew members. Female crew are not generated by default like male crew members, they instead need to be earned by completing personal missions. However, they already come with 100% in their main role and a fully trained Sisterhood of Steel perk, making them extremely powerful. You can earn 20 of them by completing the entire campaign and you can choose what nation and vehicle they're assigned to. As such they're an excellent way to get a really good crew. Start working towards them right away and stockpile them for when you hit Tier IV or V tanks.

XP, CREDITS AND GOLD

A guide to the various currencies of World of Tanks, how to earn them and, most importantly, what to spend them on.

In World of Tanks there are three main types of currency. Experience is used to unlock new tanks and upgrades in your tech tree, Credits are used to purchase those tanks and modules (as well as equipment, consumables, ammo and lots of other things) and Gold is bought with real money and used to purchase high quality items.

EXPERIENCE

Experience is earned by competing in battles. There are two kinds of experience:

• 95% of the experience you earn is regular experience. This is tied to the vehicle you earn it in and cannot be transferred.

• 5% of the experience you earn is free experience. This is not tied to a specific vehicle and can be used on any vehicle you want. It is often used to immediately purchase upgrades for new tanks that have poor starting modules. You can convert regular experience to free experience by spending gold (this is explained in more detail later in this chapter).

CREDITS

Credits are earned in game by competing in battles. The majority of transactions in the game are credit based. You will be earning and spending credits constantly in order to repair, reload and upgrade your tanks, as well as buy equipment, consumables and other items.

Here's the full list of ways in which you can earn XP and credits:

ACTION	XP	CREDITS
Join a battle	✗	✓
Spotting an enemy for the first time	✓	✓
Damaging an enemy tank	✓	✓
Team member damages tank you spotted	✓	✓
Destroying a module on any enemy tank	✓	✗
Knocking out an enemy crew member	✓	✗
Kill shot on enemy vehicle	✓	✓
Knock out last crew member on vehicle	✓	✓
Attempt to capture base	✓	✗
Fully capture base	✓	✓
Defend base	✓	✗
Survive battle	✓	✗
Loss	✗	✗
Draw	✗	✗
Victory	✓	✓
Damaged by own team*	✗	✓

*Note: if you are the one who damages another player on your team you take a penalty hit on credits earned.

Credits and experience can also be offered as a reward for completing missions or events, along with crew experience, days of premium or even whole tanks.

You can dramatically increase the amount of credits and experience you earn by using one of two ways to multiply your income:

A PREMIUM ACCOUNT earns you 1.5x credits and experience. You can buy days, weeks or months of premium by spending gold, just as you might subscribe to an MMO.

YOUR FIRST WIN OF THE DAY in a vehicle earns you 2x experience (but no bonus credits). To utilise this, you'll want to make sure you win at least once a day in each vehicle that you own, and hope you put in a good performance when you do. There's nothing as frustrating as dying instantly only for your team to go on and win, wasting your multiplier.

GOLD

Gold is the premium currency that is bought with real world money. Gold is used in a limited number of high value transactions such as purchasing premium tanks or consumables. Gold can occasionally be acquired for free via promotions or earned via events and clan wars. As a general rule if something can be bought by gold it is likely much better than its credit based counterpart, but one must take the cost into consideration.

Here's how you can spend your money on World of Tanks:

PREMIUM ACCOUNT – Buying premium gives you a 1.5x multiplier to all experience and credits earned, making it the best way to accelerate your levelling up.

PREMIUM TANK – Premium tanks are cheap to repair and reload, making them better at making money a lot better than their standard counterparts. They're also very useful for training crew, and some of them are just plain fun to drive. Buying a decent Tier V-VIII premium tank can be a good way to earn credits, and unlike a premium account, you get to keep it forever.

GARAGE SLOTS – If you plan to have a lot of tanks, sooner or later you're going to need to make space for them. Having several tanks on the go allows you to maximize the first win bonus.

COMPLEX EQUIPMENT – Complex equipment costs a lot of credits, but de-mounting it costs only a tiny amount of gold. Well worth it.

CREW TRAINING – At high levels having a 100% crew is a must. While some 100% crew members can be earned through missions, if you run out you'll need to spend money.

BARRACKS SLOTS – Same deal as the garage expansion, sooner or later you will need more bunks.

CAMO SKINS – Camo skins look cool, but they can also give you a bonus to your camouflage rating. If you have a favourite tank destroyer this can be worth the investment.

CONVERT EXPERIENCE TO FREE EXPERIENCE – When you've maxed out the research tree for a tank (or if you're using a premium tank), you gain the ability to convert experience earned by that tank to free experience at a rate of one gold per 25 XP.

PREMIUM AMMO – Premium ammunition is usually better than standard ammo, but you can burn through gold quickly by using it. It is probably only wise to use this if you have a tank that benefits very well from premium ammo, and even then consider using credits to buy it instead (you can choose between gold and credit purchase of premium ammo).

PREMIUM CONSUMABLES – The same deal as premium ammo. You're generally better off using credits to buy these.

CONVERT GOLD TO CREDITS – Premium accounts and premium tanks are a much better method of generating credits in the long run, but this is a useful method if you really need credits in a hurry.

XP EARNING

To level up and unlock the best and coolest tanks you're going to need both experience and credits. Here are my top tips for getting your hands on them.

KEEP A SCHEDULE

As I explained in the last chapter, netting your first win of the day awards a sizable bonus, doubling all experience earned for that battle. As a result the best way to earn experience is to play every day and stick at it at least long enough to net a win. Remember too that the first match bonus applies to each tank individually, so be sure to push down several tank lines at once, scoring a win with each one every day.

GET PREMIUM

I really can't emphasise this enough, the best way to farm experience is to do so with a premium account. A 1.5x multiplier for all experience and credits is just huge. It's one of the most cost effective ways to spend money on World of Tanks, so just make sure you're playing regularly while your premium subscription is active.

TEAM UP

Most random battles are chaotic and disorganized, especially on the lower tiers. If you've got a friend to play with, platoon up and get on voice chat. Two tanks of the same class working together have a huge advantage in the average public game, and you should be able to score plenty of kills. When one of you damages a tank the other one spotted first, you both get experience!

SURVIVE

Surviving a battle nets you an XP bonus. Surviving a battle without taking much damage will save you money in experience costs. Thus if you find yourself hopelessly outmatched, the only tank left alive against four or five enemies, it's in your best interests to hide and allow them to capture your base rather than fighting a losing battle.

CAPTURE THAT POINT

On the other side of the coin, if the sole remaining enemy is hiding to prevent you from finishing them off, don't worry about chasing them down, head to the enemy base and capture it. Each tank that captures the point will get an experience bonus, so don't be shy, race in there to grab your share of the spoils!

BE AGGRESSIVE

While it's better to survive a battle if you can, playing too cautiously can waste your time. If you've got a decent credit-farming tank then repair costs shouldn't bother you too much, so it's better to destroy a couple of tanks and face destruction yourself in a five-minute blaze of glory than survive a whole session while dealing no damage. Not only do you get more experience, you can play three games in the time a cautious player might spend in one!

SPOTTING

Spotting is one of the most under-appreciated parts of World of Tanks. Not only is it a necessary part of winning games, it gets you experience too! Being the first person to spot a tank gets you experience, and you also get experience if one of your teammates damages the tank you're spotting. What this means is that it is useful to keep enemy tanks in view, even if you can't take them out yourself. Rather than charging in wildly, continue reporting their position and hope your artillery takes the hint.

SUICIDE SCOUTING

I touched on this during the first battle tips. Since you get experience for being the first person to spot an enemy tank, one way to gain experience in a poor tank is to drive directly at the enemy, spot them all, and instantly get destroyed. This only gets you a small amount of experience, but it doesn't take very long either. Just don't expect to make many friends this way, as you're not really helping your teammates by taking a dive.

MISSIONS

World of Tanks is full of missions, events and daily targets, all of which will reward you with various things like experience, credits, days of premium or premium tanks (the latter of which can be used to farm the former). So keeping an eye on your missions tab is a great way to get ahead. You don't do missions automatically, you have to manually accept them and turn them in, so keep an eye on your missions tab and constantly get involved in missions to gain extra rewards.

SPEND YOUR WAY TO THE TOP

If you really find yourself struggling to make an impact, you can always buy yourself an edge. Premium consumables and ammo can give you significant boosts when it comes to damaging enemy tanks. I recommend chocolate, or your closest national equivalent, for an all around combat boost.

THE BIGGER THE BETTER

The higher the level of the tank you damage, the more experience you get, so the best way to get experience is to hurt a tank much higher level than you. Obviously that's easier said than done, but even if you struggle to inflict major damage on a high level tank, you still might be able to shoot out its tracks for a quick boost of XP.

THE BEST CREDIT FARMING TANKS

Getting experience is only half the battle, to level up you'll need to farm credits, and the best way to do that is in a premium tank.

CHURCHILL III

A cost-effective option at 1,500 gold, the Churchill III is an excellent credit-farming tank, known for its low upkeep costs. In a good match the Churchill can earn tens of thousands of credits, and it also acts as an excellent crew trainer for your Soviet tanks. It's only Tier V, so it'll be out-earned by most of the other tanks on this list, but it's by far the cheapest option.

DICKER MAX

The Dicker Max is a German tank destroyer with an emphasis on sniping. It deals significant damage from relative safety, but costs more than twice as much as the Churchill at 3,200 gold.

SU-122-44

Double the price of the Dicker Max and you'll end up in the market for a 6,750-gold SU-122-44, a Soviet tank destroyer that can mix it up surprisingly well on the front lines. The SU-122-44 consistently penetrates the armour of level 8 and 9 tanks, making it a great credit earner.

T34

Not to be confused with the Soviet T-34, the T34 is a Tier VIII US tank, which is widely acknowledged as the best tier for making money. However, Tier VIII premium tanks cost a lot, with a T34 setting you back 12,000 gold. However, if you buy it, learn how to play it effectively and if you use it regularly you'll never need to worry about credits again.

BATTLE TYPES AND MODES

There are various types of battles in World of Tanks. You are unlikely to see many of them at the beginning, but this section will supply you with all the information you need to start winning crucial battles as soon as possible.

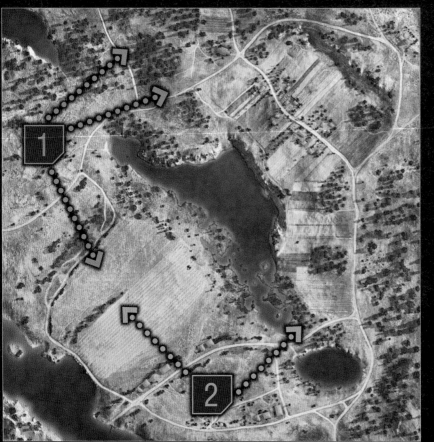

STANDARD BATTLE

Two teams of 15 players start at opposite sides of a map, each with a base for their team. They then have fifteen minutes to either capture the opponent's home base or destroy all tanks on the other team. If none of these goals are met when the time runs out the game ends in a draw.

Standard Battle is the default game mode for World of Tanks and can be played on all maps.

ENCOUNTER

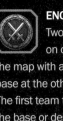

Two teams start on one side of the map with a neutral base at the other end. The first team to capture the base or destroy all the enemy tanks wins. If neither of these goals are met in 15 minutes the match is a draw.

Encounter is available on a limited number of maps, but many more than Assault.

ASSAULT

Two teams of 15 start at opposite sides of the map, but only one team has a base that can be captured. The attacking team must capture that base or destroy all the defenders within 10 minutes or the defenders win.

Assault is currently only available on a very small number of maps.

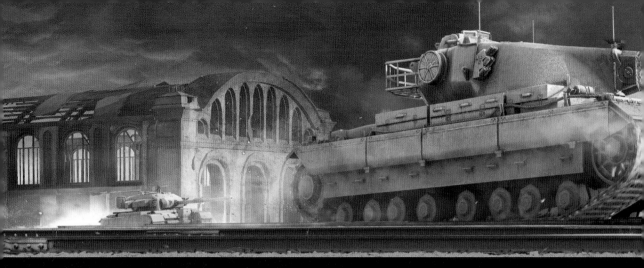

MODES

RANDOM BATTLE

This is what you get put into when you click the big red 'Battle' button at the top of the screen. A random battle sorts you into either a Standard Battle (60% chance), Assault (20% chance) or Encounter Battle (20% chance). There is an option in Settings to disable the ability to be matched into Assault or Encounter Battles and play exclusively Standard Battles instead.

Whichever kind of battle you end up in you'll be sorted into two teams of 15 random players and sorted onto a randomly selected map. The vehicles will generally be within four vehicle tiers of one another due to the matchmaker, which sorts each tank according to specific priorities.

Random Battles will earn you credits and experience depending on how well you perform in battles early on. You'll spend most of your time in World of Tanks playing Random Battles, at least at the very beginning anyway.

NEWCOMER BATTLE

New players (those in Tier I and II tanks) are redirected into a special version of Random Battle where they only play on a limited number of maps while they get familiar with the game.

PLATOONS

Up to three players can join together in a platoon. This means that they'll be matchmade into the same game, on the same team. Your platoon members are highlighted a different colour in game to make them easy to find. Beware of creating platoons with more than three levels difference between player vehicles, as the lower level player will be matchmade into a high level game and struggle to make any impact.

TEAM BATTLE

Team Battle is sometimes referred to as players as "7/54" because each team consists of seven players and a maximum of 54 tier "points" (a Tier V tank is worth five points, a Tier VI tank is worth six points, etc). Vehicles must be at least Tier VI to take part, and cannot be higher than Tier VIII, but there are many combinations of tanks possible within those restrictions.

Team Battle requires a lot more organisation and co-ordination than Random Battle. It represents the more e-sports orientated aspect of the game. Accordingly, it uses a matchmaker based on player skill, rather than tank tier. There is also a ranked version for permanent teams of up to 12 players (with seven eligible to play in each match).

In addition to the usual battle types, Team Battle features a two flag assault mode in which the defenders must defend two different capture points.

TEAM TRAINING

Training is a custom battle mode where you can create your own match and select your own map. You can make your battle public or just invite friends. This is useful for players trying to learn the game or try out new tanks and maps. You do not earn credits or experience in this mode and repairs are free.

TANK COMPANY BATTLE

Another points based team battle mode. There are four divisions of Tank Company: Junior, Medium, Champion and Absolute. Each one has its own tier and point restrictions, which work similarly to Team Battle:

JUNIOR

Minimum 20 pts – maximum 40 pts

Artillery level 2–4

Tank destroyer level 2–4

Light tank level 1–3

Medium tank level 2–4

Heavy tank level 4

MEDIUM

Minimum 40 pts – maximum 60 pts

Artillery level 2–6

Tank destroyer level 2–6

Light tank level 1–4

Medium tank level 2–6

Heavy tank level 4–6

CHAMPION

Minimum 60 pts – maximum 90 pts

Artillery level 2–8

Tank destroyer level 2–8

Light tank level 1–8

Medium tank level 2–8

Heavy tank level 4–8

ABSOLUTE

Minimum 90 pts – maximum 150 pts

Artillery level 2–10

Tank destroyer level 2–10

Light tank level 1–10

Medium tank level 1–10

Heavy tank level 4–10

CLAN WARS

Clan Wars a high level guild vs guild form of combat that employs a turn-based strategic map to provide context to battles. You can read about Clan Wars in detail on page 190.

STRONGHOLDS

Strongholds is a different type of clan based warfare that allows clan members to quickly play battles against other clans without worrying about the strategic overmap. You can read about it in detail in the Clan Wars section on page 167.

REMOVED GAME MODES

HISTORICAL BATTLE

Historical Battles were a variant of standard battles that used specific scenarios inspired by great tank battles throughout history. Only specific tanks that were suitable for that battle were permitted to join. Unfortunately real history was not very well balanced, and historical battles struggled to stay competitive. It was removed in the 9.2 update for reworking.

CONFRONTATION BATTLE

Confrontation Battle was a type of random battle in which each team consisted solely of vehicles from a single nation. China and Japan were excluded due to having only a small number of tanks available. This was removed in update 9.0 due to balance issues, as some nations proved to be extremely good at countering others.

SETTINGS

There are a lot of settings to adjust in World of Tanks. Some of them will be familiar and self-explanatory, but others require a little more explanation. Here's a rundown of what settings are important and how you can tweak them to get the most out of your game.

GENERAL

1. These control your chat functions, turning on profanity filters, managing friend requests, etc.

7. Marks of excellence are symbols painted on your gun barrel if you're one of the top players for average damage in a tank type. If you have these you're probably way too advanced for this guide!

6. Autosaves a replay of your game to the replays folder in your World of Tanks directory.

3. The dynamic camera shakes when firing, but enables stabilization in sniper mode. It is useful for sniping on the move.

5. Adds a ton of useful information to the minimap, such as vehicle names. Turn it on.

2. This allows you to turn off Assault and Encounter battle options in Random Battle mode.

4. The server reticle shows you where you're actually aiming on the game servers, rather than where your client thinks you're aiming. This is useful if you have lag from a poor connection.

SCREEN

1. General graphics options. If you've played a PC game before you probably know what these mean.

2. Triple buffering does complicated computery things to speed up your game. Turn it on if you can.

3. Automatically adjusts the FoV depending on how zoomed in you are.

4. Determines how much of the screen the HUD takes up.

5. Lets you put various post processing filters on your game, including 1940s film mode!

DETAILS

1. Shadows take a major toll on your game performance. Turn them down if you need the boost.

2. Draw distance is how far out you can see objects. Turn it up as high as your PC can handle.

SOUND

1. Adjust the levels of different sound types, music, sound effects, engine noise, etc.

2. Turn on and tweak voice chat. Be sure to check your mic levels before the game starts!

2. Everyone has a preference when it comes to mouse inversion. Reverse inversion governs what happens when you're moving backwards.

1. Read the keyboard shortcuts! There are useful things in here (e.g. space for emergency stop). Feel free to remap them, especially if your mouse has more than two buttons.

3. Adjust to taste. Generally you'll want less sensitivity in sniper mode for fine aiming.

Settings

General | Graphics | Sound | Controls | Reticle | Marker

Keyboard

Move

Forward	W
Back	S
Left	A
Right	D
Lock Hull (SPGs, Tank Destroyers)	X

Cruise Control

Forward	R
Back	F
Stop and Fire	Space

Fire

Mouse

Sensitivity

Arcade Aim

Sniper Aim

Artillery Aim

☐ Horizontal inversion
☐ Vertical inversion

☐ Reverse inversion

Default

OK | Cancel | Apply

1. The gun marker is a very useful option. When set to "show penetration" it changes from red to yellow to green depending on how likely you are to penetrate armour. All tanks have weak spots, and this will help you find them.

2. Change your targeting reticle to a shape you prefer.

RETICLE

1. Decides what information you see on your HUD about each tank. By default most information is hidden unless you press alt.

2. You can set this separately for allies, enemies and destroyed tanks.

MARKER

LIGHT TANKS

Unless you're playing in the early tiers when nearly everyone is using them, light tanks are notoriously fragile and struggle to damage their bigger brothers. What they lack in toughness and firepower however, they make up for in speed and agility, making them the premier scouts of World of Tanks. Here are my top tips for playing as a light tank.

RADIO

Most light tanks are scouts, and scouts need radios. Radio Range is one of the most neglected parts of World of Tanks. It dictates the distance at which a tank can contact allies and relay spotted positions to them. Most light tanks should be investing heavily in radios and radio-related skills.

DON'T STRAY TOO FAR

As a light tank you'll be much faster than your comrades, but this comes at a risk. A light tank that advances too far forward will be out of radio range, becoming useless to their team. Instead, wait and allow your team to advance before darting ahead. Be prepared to double back behind your lines and advance again on a different flank. You're fast enough to get away with it!

THE ART OF SPOTTING

Much of what you'll do as a light tank is spotting. When you see another tank, don't charge headlong at it (unless it's another light). Alternatively, try and stay out of sight, or on the move, and relay its position back to your team, calling down artillery fire upon it.

HIT THOSE TRACKS

As a light tank you'll struggle to cause major damage to large tanks, but you can still hit their tracks and immobilise them. Couple this with effective spotting and you'll be feeding kills directly to your artillery.

RAMMING

Though it may seem counterintuitive, some light tanks can get away with ramming. The well-armoured VK 16.02 Leopard is one example. Don't ram heavy tanks, obviously, instead build up speed and hit that pesky artillery with your full momentum.

CAMOUFLAGE

Light tanks are unique in World of Tanks. Usually when a vehicle moves its camouflage value is reduced by half, light tanks do not have this penalty, they are as invisible while moving as they are standing still! As a result, a camouflage net can be a good investment on a light tank.

CIRCLE STRAFING

As a light tank you will often struggle to penetrate front armour. Fortunately you are fast enough to get to the much more vulnerable rear and side armour of other tanks. One classic strategy is to use the 'auto-aim' function (right click on a tank) and drive in rapid circles around it faster than it can track you, firing all the way.

FAVOURED TARGETS

Artillery are the prime targets for light tanks. If you find yourself breaking through the enemy lines, go hunting for their self-propelled guns, whose armour will be easy prey to your weapons. Beware though as Artillery can fire off powerful 'no scope' shots, so don't approach head on unless you know they're reloading. Tank destroyers also make good targets, as their lack of turrets mean they'll struggle to turn to face you.

COUNTER SCOUTING

There are some light tanks that don't have the radio to make good scouts. Some of those are 'light mediums' (below) but others just aren't very good at scouting. These are best put to use running down and destroying enemy scouts that try and break through your lines. One you've achieved that, head for their artillery!

THE LIGHT MEDIUM

Not every tank fits into a designated role. Some nations, such as Britain and Japan, have light tanks that work less like scouts and more like smaller medium tanks. The hallmark of a light medium is usually a poor radio, but good armour and/or HP. They should generally be played as you would a medium tank (see overleaf), while taking advantage of their extra agility and camouflage.

COUNTERING LIGHT TANKS

The main weapon of the light tank is speed and manoeuvrability. You can never hope to out-drive a light tank, unless you have one of your own, however you can easily outgun it.

In combat a light tank is likely to try and circle around behind you to shoot at your vulnerable rear armour, so it is vital to have a fast turning turret that can keep up with them. Gun penetration is not a priority when dealing with light tanks, nor is outright damage. Instead you should focus on smaller guns that aim and fire rapidly. When a light tank is zig-zagging across the battlefield you're likely to miss a couple of shots, so it is wise to be able to shoot again quickly!

The best counter to a light tank is a medium or heavy tank with decent armour or high HP, a fast turning turret and a light, rapid firing gun. Light tanks will struggle to damage it, while its gun can quickly follow their movement and destroy them. Oddly, speed is not that necessary, as if the scouts are running away you have done your job! These tanks should be positioned on the flanks of an advance, guarding well known scout paths to ensure the team isn't flanked. While taking out the tracks of a light tank makes it vulnerable, it often isn't necessary as many will die in one hit regardless.

MEDIUM TANKS

Medium tanks are exceptionally versatile and capable of fulfilling a number of roles on the battlefield, which is why this section features a lot of different tactics. Some medium tanks may fill only one of these roles, while others might be capable of doing several, some tanks can even do all of them! It all boils down to knowing what your tank is good at and what your team needs.

FLANKER

Flankers are medium tanks that have particularly good speed, but perhaps lack in the armour department. They drive similiar to light tanks without the priority on scouting, running quickly down the flanks to get shots at rear and side armour. Flankers will often use high damage, low penetration guns to quickly deliver a killing blow to rear or side armour. Autoloaders are particularly popular due to their ability to deliver a lot of damage in a short space of time, followed by a retreat.

BRAWLER

Particularly well armoured medium tanks will take on a 'brawler' role, playing a lot like more mobile heavy tanks, going toe-to-toe with enemies to contest objectives. Don't play exactly like a heavy tank though, instead look for objectives further afield, or uphill, that slower tanks will struggle to get to. Be aggressive, and use your speed to

get right into the faces of tanks that would prefer to keep their distance.

SUPPORT

A support medium is one that generally equips a good gun, but lacks a little in speed or armour. Generally speaking these tanks should follow behind heavy tanks or brawler mediums and shoot over their 'shoulder' at enemies. Think of heavy tanks as small mobile buildings, and use them as you would any other piece of cover. One especially useful tactic is to wait for the enemy tank to fire at your big buddy, then pop out and fire your shots while they're busy reloading.

SNIPER

Some medium tanks include extremely accurate, long range guns and prefer to deploy far back behind their own lines and snipe. Much like the 'light mediums' on the previous page, these tanks behave more like sniper tank destroyers so skip to that section to learn more.

BREAKING THROUGH

Often as a medium tank you will find yourself close to the front lines, only to see a gap appear that the enemy isn't covering. If you have the speed you can race through that gap and arrive in the enemy deployment zone, capturing their base and attacking their artillery. This forces them into a hard choice, ignore you and let you create havoc, or turn around and expose their rear to your allies. Just know you're taking a gamble when you do this, sometimes those 'gaps' are actually covered by hidden snipers.

WOLFPACK

As I mentioned in the first Battle Roll Out section, medium tanks are at their best when they roll in groups (three works well). At the beginning, you'll just want to follow the crowd, but in later battles you'll want to use the chat functions to pro-actively organise some teammates. If you have a friend or two to play with, organising a medium tank wolfpack is a good way to start. Wolfpacks can consist of similar tanks, such as a group of brawlers rushing an objective together, or a mixed group, such as a support tank hiding behind two sturdier friends. Ideally though they should be roughly the same speed, so no-one is left behind.

REPAIR

Having your tracks broken is a death sentence for medium tanks, so investing in the repair skill is vitally important. A high repair skill means your tracks will be repaired quicker, while repair kits can fix them instantly. Both are a wise and practical investment.

COUNTERING MEDIUM TANKS

Most medium tanks rely on mobility rather than armour or hitpoints for protection, so it's vitally important to slow them down by hitting them in the tracks. This can also serve the function of splitting up a wolfpack, by hobbling one member, forcing the others to either press on or slow down to cover for their friend. Numbers are the big advantage medium tanks have, do not engage several of them without support, unless you're riding in a hitpoint monster like a TOG II.

Attacking a medium tank with a great big howitzer isn't a great idea, it's inefficient and the long reload times will mean you'll struggle to hit fast moving targets (unless they've been immobilized). Instead, you'll be looking for a decent medium size gun with a good rate of fire and AP ammo to help overcome the sloped armour that a lot of medium tanks use.

Remember to prioritize targets – the biggest guns on your team will be going after heavy tanks – so those with less impressive firepower should thin out the mediums. One of the best weapons medium tanks have is being underestimated, if an entire team focus fires on the biggest target, a group of mediums will tear you to shreds. Guarding your flanks is also vitally important when dealing with medium tanks. They will try and get behind heavy tanks to attack from the rear, so it is important to support your main battle line with tanks specifically tasked to watching and guarding the flanks.

HEAVY TANKS

Heavy tanks are the anchor of a team. They are expected to hold chokepoints, spearhead assaults and slowly push back the enemy. They have the strongest armour and can wreak serious carnage – they are the masters of close quarters fighting – but they have their weaknesses too...

TOUGH IT OUT

As a heavy tank, you're likely to get damaged several times before you actually get taken out of action. As a result, you'll want to invest a lot more in anything that lets you continue functioning after you get hit. Mostly this means the repair skill and repair kits, but it can also mean things like the recon skill, which compensates for a damaged viewfinder.

PACE YOURSELF

While some heavy tanks can move quickly enough to steal tactics from the brawler medium playbook, others are much, much slower. Riding in a slow tank force you'll need to make a decision as to where you're going to go and rigidly stick to it. Do not go on long flanking journeys and avoid steep hills. Anything that takes you out of the fighting for an extended period is probably a bad idea.

RAMMING

As a heavy tank you have the ability to bully opposing tanks physically, pushing them around to rearrange the battlefield to your tastes. Don't be afraid to go on ramming rampages against smaller tanks, even if you don't connect, you'll force them to retreat.

CHOKEPOINT

Pick your battlefield carefully. Heavy tanks are at their best in enclosed spaces where they can't be easily flanked and can force enemies to attack their strong front armour. Thus your tank will be far more effective in a city fight, where the tanks are funnelled into place by narrow streets.

AGROPHOBIA

By contrast you'll want to avoid wide open spaces, as this will allow tank destroyers and artillery to have clear sightlines to you, while medium and light tanks can simply out run you. Only venture into the open field in the late game, when other important areas are won.

PRIORITY TARGETS

Heavy tanks with particularly big guns (I'm looking at you KV-2) have to be very disciplined in how and when they fire. While obliterating a vulnerable light tank may be good for your kill/death ratio, it might not be a good choice if you're using a large, slow to reload cannon. Not only will you likely miss against such a nimble target, but that shot could instead have been used on a much more threatening heavy tank. The slow and ponderous nature of heavy tanks makes picking your battles important.

YOU ARE COVER

As explained in the medium tank section, heavy tanks can often be thought of as a kind of mobile cover. As an heavy tank driver it is important to be aware of this. Protect the squishy mediums hiding behind you, make sure they understand where you're going, either using chat or by telegraphing your movements. Try to avoid sudden moves that might expose them.

PEEK-A-BOOM

When engaging in a street fight you shouldn't just park in the middle of the street and let yourself get shot. Alternatively, play 'peek-a-boom': keep your tank hidden behind a corner, and pop out to fire and retreat to reload. This is a strong way of holding a chokepoint until you're ready to push.

ADVANCED TACTICS

In addition to playing peek-a-boom heavy tanks are particularly adept at using the hull down, sidescraping and facehugging tactics described on page 90. Read up on these techniques if you are committed to playing as a heavy tank.

KNOW WHEN TO PUSH

It's easy to get suckered into playing a long game of peek-a-boom when driving a heavy, holding a location but never

COUNTERING HEAVY TANKS

Heavy tanks are capable of standing toe-to-toe with any tank in the game, so the best way to deal with them is to deny them that opportunity. Their main threats are flanking medium tanks who attack their rear armour, well-armed tank destroyers who can attack them from range, and of course artillery.

The latter deserves special attention, heavy tanks are excellent targets for artillery commanders as their lack of speed makes them easy to hit. Thus medium and light tank drivers should give priority to surviving and continuing to report the heavy tank's position, leaving it open to bombardment.

It is important to know when and where to engage heavy tanks. Do not start a street fight with one if you don't have to, instead surrender the ground and lure your enemy out in the wide open areas, where they are vulnerable.

TANK DESTROYERS

Tank destroyers are typically the "snipers" of World of Tanks, mounting large, slow-firing guns by making compromises elsewhere. Lower level tank destroyers will rely on stealth and long range to keep themselves safe, while high tanks often come with extremely heavy armour. Either way their job is to target the toughest tanks the enemy has to offer and take them out.

SNIPING

Many tank destroyers, especially in at the lower tiers, will rely on sniping and ambush tactics. In order to mount their oversized guns tanks destroyers will generally sacrifice speed, armour, turning ability or a turret, so they don't thrive on the front lines. Instead engage foes at range, look for forests and cliff edges with good vantage points over the battlefield. Remember the routes you took and search for spots that overlook them.

THE HEAVY TANK DESTROYER

In the upper tiers many tank destroyer lines transition between lightly armoured ambush tanks to heavily armoured behemoths. Such large vehicles will struggle

to hide themselves effectively, relying more on their thick armour to keep them safe. Naturally this encourages players to sit closer to the front lines, but beware! A heavy tank destroyer's lack of a turret can be difficult in the close quarters fighting heavy tanks favour. Instead consider following heavy tanks into battle but hanging back a little from them, finding a place with good sight lines and staying put. Don't overmanoeuvre.

CAMOUFLAGE

Camouflage is very important to tank destroyers, who typically try and hide in a good sniper spot for the majority of the battle. They are the premier users of camouflage nets (light tanks come second, but tend to move about too much to make full use of one). If you have a favourite tank destroyer you should consider investing in a skin to increase its camouflage value. Any bonus you can get to staying hidden is one you should take.

HUNTING HEAVIES

Tank destroyers typically bring some of the biggest guns to the field, many of which are slow to aim and reload. This is only exacerbated by their general lack of turrets, giving them real trouble tracking a moving target. So unless you happen to possess one of the more fast firing tank destroyer guns, you should focus your effort on slow, well armoured tanks who are easier to hit and a more efficient use of your firepower. Thus your priority targets should be heavy tanks and tank destroyers, with medium tanks considered only when you can't find one of those.

SHOOT AND SCOOT

As with all games, playing the "sniper" can lead people to camp in one spot excessively. I've definitely witnessed games where half the team drove a mere 200m from their spawn point and all sat in the first sniper spot they came up to. Not only is this inefficient (six guns covering one sight line instead of one gun covering six sight lines) it's also more dangerous than it looks. Experienced players know exactly where these 'newbie friendly' sniper spots are, and know just how to drop an artillery strike on one. To mix things up, I advocate a "shoot and scoot" approach, where tank destroyers change position every few shots, preventing the enemy from zeroing in on your location.

OVERWATCH

It's important to remember that as a tank destroyer your job is not merely to destroy the enemy, but to protect your allies as well. No matter how good you are you'll struggle to win a game without some more mobile tanks to take the capture point for you. Thus it's important to watch your allies through your scope, and prioritize targets they are engaged with. Helpfully this is also a great way to score kills, as your allies will be distracting, inflicting damage and

COUNTERING TANK DESTROYERS

Sniper destroyers are best dealt with by light tanks, who can penetrate deep behind enemy lines and spot them, making them vulnerable to artillery fire. Heavy destroyers on the other hand are best treated like heavy tanks, only with limited manoeuvrability.

Most tank destroyers do not have turrets (and those that do often have slow turret traverse speed), and this can be used to your advantage. Instead of assaulting a tank destroyer head on, drive past it and then turn, running circles around it while firing repeatedly. With no turret to track you the tank destroyer will be forced to turn on the spot, and will likely not be able to do so fast enough to get you in its sights.

One advanced tactic for dealing with tank destroyers is to go track to track. By pressing the side of your tank up against the destroyers tracks you can render both vehicles unable to turn. At that point you can simply turn your turret and fire into their side armour with impunity.

ARTILLERY

So far we haven't spoken that much about artillery. This is because they play a very different game to anyone else. Artillery players use an overhead map instead of a zoom function, and require no line of sight on their targets. This makes them highly dependent on their teammates to spot enemies for them. But when they get that satisfying target lock, they can unleash a devastating cascade of firepower aimed at vulnerable top armour.

THE OVERHEAD MAP

A friend of mine once described the artillery game in World of Tanks as a point and click adventure game where the solution to every puzzle is 'use shell on tank'. It's a very different viewpoint from the regular game, and requires a different approach. It's easy to get disconnected from your tank while looking at the greater battlefield. So make sure you un-zoom now and again to re-orientate yourself.

FIRING ARCS

A major part of playing as artillery is understanding firing arcs. Artillery that fires in a high arc is able to get up and over cover, hitting vehicles pressing up against walls. Those with flatter arcs will struggle to achieve this and will need to target those vehicles more out in the open.

SPLASH DAMAGE

Artillery is notoriously inaccurate, but makes up for that by not requiring a direct hit, instead it inflicts damage in an area around the target. This is important to understand when playing as artillery partly because it helps you hit your target, but also to ensure you don't accidentally hit your allies!

NO SCOPE

Artillery is not completely defenceless in direct fire. If they don't go to the overhead map, they are capable of firing "from the hip" in the same way as a tank destroyer with no zoom ability. It's a hard shot to aim, but destructive when it lands. Just don't miss, you'll be dead before you reload.

WHERE TO HIDE

Finding a good artillery spot is similar to finding a good sniper spot, both place a priority on remaining hidden and still. The difference is that artillery don't require a line of sight for their target, but they do require a clear sky – standing next to a cliff is no good! Forests make the best hiding spots. Unlike snipers I don't really recommend artillery 'shoot and scoot' too much, as their main defence is that their targets usually don't have line of sight to them, so moving would just expose them.

WAIT FOR THE SIGNAL

Artillery, more than any other vehicle, is dependent on their team. If they don't spot tanks you have nothing to shoot at. For the most part spotting is supported within the game itself, and enemies will be highlighted on your map. Sometimes, however, a player doesn't spot an enemy but can still make an educated guess as to where they are, in this instance they'll hopefully ping the map or type something in chat to call down fire, so make sure you're paying attention.

MAKE IT COUNT

Artillery suffers from some of the longest reload times in the game, astronomically long in some cases. You don't want to be shooting at half chances (unless the game has just started, as below), make sure you have a good chance before you fire – you'll be kicking yourself if a better opportunity comes up while you're busy reloading.

KILL THE CAMPER

As I mentioned in the tank destroyer section, there are certain parts of every map that are popular newbie sniping points, usually ones near the deployment zone. Learn them, then when the game starts drop a shell right on them to discourage the other team. If you're fast enough you can land it and still reload before the rest of your team makes contact with the enemy.

GIANT KILLER

Much like heavy tanks and tank destroyers, artillery need to prioritise their targets. Light tanks are a poor choice, as they

COUNTERING ARTILLERY

Artillery isn't hard to destroy, armour is almost an afterthought for them. The trick is finding and getting to them, as they generally lurk in cover behind enemy lines. Light tanks are the best at attacking artillery, combining their high speed and stealth to slip through the lines and detect hidden guns. Artillery are one of the few targets soft enough for light tanks to take on without backup, just watch out for the "no scope" shot.

Avoiding artillery fire is also important. There's a few main ways to do this. The first is to make use of camouflage to avoid being spotted in the first place, the second is to move quickly and unpredictably in order to make yourself hard to hit, and the third is to "hug the wall" and make it difficult for flat arc artillery to land a shell on you.

Above all, the prime directive when facing artillery is "Don't stay still".

are far too quick and nimble for you to reliably hit, and best handled by others. Concentrate fire on heavy tanks, who move slowly, and tank destroyers, who like to stay still for long periods, instead. The latter are especially vulnerable to artillery fire, as many of them are open topped.

TACTICS BY TIER

The matchmaking system in World of Tanks is incredibly complicated. To explain it all might require another book! Sufficed to say that just because you're in a Tier III tank doesn't mean you'll only fight other Tier III tanks. You might be matched into battles containing Tier IV or even (rarely) Tier V tanks as the runt of the litter or you might get matched into a Tier II battle as top dog. If that happens... make the most of it!

Even more confusingly, some tanks, such as artillery and dedicated scouts, get matchmade into higher tier games as a matter of course. The tactics here are presented as what you can expect to see when you press "random battle" while using a regular tank of that tier. That means that even though the first heavy tanks appear at Tier IV and V, I warn you to be on the look-out for them at Tier III, because that's when you hypothetically might start getting put into games with them. Good luck!

TIER I

Your first few battles. At this point you will mostly be matched with other new players all driving starter light tanks. First of all, make sure you've read and digested the Your First Battle Roll Out on page 28. Knowing how each class of tank should behave is not essential, as at this point almost all

the tanks you will face will be light tanks. An important note here is that you will hardly ever encounter artillery and tank destroyers, making dashing forward in the open far more rewarding. Use this opportunity to practice your flanking tactics, rather than standing and sniping.

TIER II

At this point the tanks will start to separate out into their constituent classes. You still won't be seeing any heavy tanks and medium tanks are a rarity, but you'll start to see artillery popping up occasionally at this point, so if you notice the enemy has one, start thinking more about hugging walls, zig-zagging out in the open and fleeing when spotted. Players will also be getting their first tank destroyers at this level. While experienced players will know how to use them, newbies will usually either sit just outside their base sniping at people or charge into battle just like any other tank. The latter are easy kills, as they don't realize how vulnerable their tank destroyers truly are, while the former are usually vulnerable to flanking.

TIER III

Effective immediately, tank destroyers and artillery are firmly part of the game, while medium tanks start to appear too. Go read the medium tank guide if you haven't yet. You might encounter a heavy when you're matched into a high tier game, but they should still be pretty rare. The introduction of medium tanks changes the game considerably. While things are still fast faced and fluid, the lighter tanks are now facing an opponent who can theoretically bully them, with medium brawlers taking on a role similar to heavy tanks in the later game. Light tanks can still make an impact beyond scouting though, especially if they team up and act like a group of mediums.

TIER IV

Heavy tanks are now a common sight when you're matched into higher tier battles, so take some time to read the heavy tank tactics entry now. At this point the game roles have fully coalesced, most light tanks are now full scouts, heavies duke it out at chokepoints and mediums hunt in packs. This is also the stage where previously unimportant things like skill training and equipment start to have a major impact. You should consider buying the enhanced 75% crew from the regimental school at this point. Re-usable equipment like camouflage nets, toolboxes and

binocular telescopes are also a good idea, as are repair kit consumables. This can obviously be quite a drain on your credits, and also quickly realise it is taking much longer to earn the experience to upgrade your tanks. From now on, you'll want to consider buying some days of premium, and possibly a Tier V premium tank to help you grind out credits. Hopefully by now you've identified the tank lines you're having the most fun with and plan to push forward with.

TIER V

Tier V is a good 'sweet spot' to stop and take stock of your situation. By now all the tank classes have been introduced and are fully populated. If you've been aiming for a heavy tank, you should now have it. Tier V is a fun tier to mess around in, and I keep some of my favourite Tier V tanks (like the VK 16.02 Leopard) around just to take out for a drive now and again. The next five levels are a much heavier investment than the previous five, and you should know exactly what you're aiming for if you tackle them. In particular you're probably going to have to spend money in the shape of premium accounts and money making tanks to achieve those goals. You should certainly be using at

least 75% crew now, possibly even 100% ones from the tank academy or the personal missions. You should also be using what equipment and consumables you can get your hands on. Don't be too worried about slowing down your advance by spending money on these, the investment will make it much easier to win games and earn experience in the future, plus it'll be far more fun to play.

TIER VI

Tier VI is similar to Tier VI, with tanks now firmly solidified into roles. Light tanks, for example, are now almost all dedicated scouts. You'll also start seeing some fearsomely large guns here, such as the famous KV-2 and its 152mm howitzer, capable of blasting several smaller tanks. At this point both crew experience and repair costs are becoming very important, and you'll likely be using a premium tank and dabbling in buying 100% crews for your favourite tanks.

This is also the tier at which you can start participating in Team Battles, if you've got a group of friends to play with. I recommend it, it's a lot of fun!

8

7

TIER VII

Tier VII is firmly in the same 'upper mid' territory occupied by Tiers VI & VIII. Roles are established, battles still make good money and you're eligible for many of more fun battle modes. By now you should be buying or retraining 100% crews (or close to it) for all your tanks, and making sure they're well equipped with equipment and consumables. You're going to be looking for every edge you can get to reach the promised land of Tier VIII.

TIER VIII

Like Tier V, Tier VIII represents a good break point, a time to take stock of what you've achieved and make plans for your ascent to the top. It's the biggest moneymaking tier, as beyond this point the costs of repairs start to outweigh the rewards from battles. I definitely recommend buying a premium tank at this tier to fund yourself in Tiers IX and X. This is also the highest tier which is still eligible for the excellent team battle mode, so I highly recommend keeping some of your favourite Tier VIIIs around for that. On the battlefield level this is where you'll first start encountering "late game" tactics. Specifically many tank destroyers will metamorphosis from stealthy snipers to armoured juggernauts, changing their tactics completely. There are no light tanks higher than Tier VIII, but the special matchmaking given to dedicated scouts means they will continue to pop up in Tier IX and X games.

TIER IX

Starting now you are firmly engaged in the "end game" of World of Tanks. You'll likely be alternating between your Tier IX tank and a Tier VIII premium in order to pay your high running and repair costs. Tactics-wise the "juggernaut" tank destroyer will be out in force, and the few tank destroyers that remain fragile will be equipping truly absurd guns. The lack of high level light tanks will also sometimes mean mediums get relegated to the scouting role, whilst fast heavy tanks get in on the medium action.

TIER X

Congratulations, you've made it! The highest level tanks come with all their upgrades fully unlocked, and you'll probably have the equipment and crew to take it to peak performance immediately. The grind is finally over, and all that remains is to take a victory lap.

TACTICS BY BATTLE TYPE

You are now armed with lots of general tactics for staying alive and strategies for destroying enemy tanks. This section now focuses on how to actually win each of the three main battle modes by fulfilling their complex objectives.

STANDARD BATTLE

Standard Battle is the default way of playing World of Tanks, and as such most of the general tactical advice found in other chapters applies here. The biggest difference between Standard Battle and an Assault or Encounter is that it is the only mode that forces you to balance your team between attacking and defending. While every other mode offers asks you to do one or the other Standard Battle asks you to do both simultaneously.

One of the easiest mistakes to make in Standard Battle is to assume that "defending" means camping out in your own base. Similar to defending in an Assault, this approach makes you predictable and easy to outmanoeuvre or bombard with artillery. Instead, you'll be looking to identify chokepoints and overwatch positions for your heavy tanks to hold. Mediums on the other hand should generally be using their speed to attack, but be prepared to retreat and defend their capture zone in an emergency.

Standard Battle is also the only mode in which you can get into a capture "race". That is both sides attempting to catch each other's points simultaneously. Two tanks will capture twice as fast as one, and three tanks will capture three times as fast, but more than that will have no additional effect. You can reset the enemy's capture counter by dealing any damage at all to the capturing tanks, this makes it a good time to use HE ammo – you don't have to do much damage, just a little!

ASSAULT (ATTACKING)

As an attacker you have the benefit of not having anything to defend. This may seem obvious, but it does change your tactics significantly. Holding chokepoints is useless to you, and instead your heavy tanks will be used for armoured pushes, while artillery and tank destroyers will be used to break up clusters of enemies and force them to move.

Artillery plays an important part in the attacker's game. Defenders will naturally be tempted to camp out very close to their base, defending a small front. This of course puts them close together and stuck in one place, making them excellent targets for artillery. Use your artillery to disrupt their formation and punish tanks that stick too close to one another. In order to stop you they'll be forced to launch an attack of their own.

One notable disadvantage the attackers have is that their forces will start the game spread out over a wide area. This can mean they hit the enemy line in a piecemeal and disorganized fashion, making them easy to defeat. Attackers need to use coordination and communication to quickly meet up and attack as a group, and can be caught in unawares if the defenders sally forth early in the game. Always remember that Assault is an asymmetric game. The defenders do not need to actively defeat you, they just need to not lose. The longer the conflict is drawn out the better a position the defenders are in.

ASSAULT (DEFENDING)

Defending in Assault mode is a very different game to attacking, or indeed to every other battle mode. Assault (attacking), Standard Battle and Encounter all give you a target area to attack, but Assault (defending) offers none of that, instead leaving you to your own devices.

When playing as a defender the obvious urge is to pull back, tightly encircle your territory and stay put. This has its benefits: a smaller front is easier to defend, and allows your tanks to easily support one another. However, there are severe drawbacks: by surrendering most of the field you give your opponent freedom to manoeuvre as they see fit and attack from any angle, while closely packing your own tanks together denies light and medium tanks the benefit of mobility. Most importantly, a group of closely packed stationary tanks is an incredibly tempting target for artillery, artillery that is free to manoeuvre and aim at will because the defenders are making no attempts to break through enemy lines and attack them.

Thus it is important not to cede the field completely, but to attack as well as defend, threatening the enemy and forcing them to react. In particular harrying artillery is going to be very important, so you must be sure to send your light tanks out to spot them.

The attacking team's main weakness is that they will be spread out at the start of the game. This means they can attack from multiple directions, but also spreads their power widely. Thus a small pack of aggressive mediums can push out and isolate individual attacking tanks, taking them out and earning you a numerical advantage. Heavy tanks and tank destroyers on the other hand should focus on the defensive effort. But they don't necessarily have to sit in their own capture zone, look for strong choke points on paths into your base and hold them.

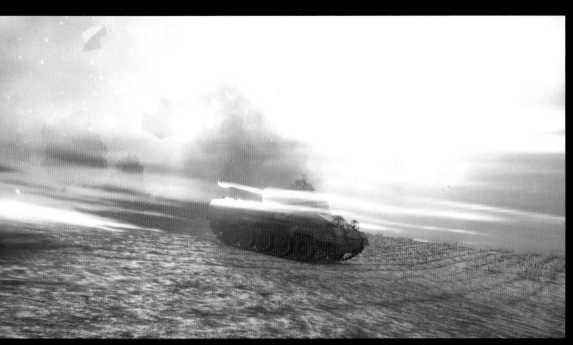

ENCOUNTER

Encounter's single capture point is usually located in the middle of the map, which means that a match will play very differently from a Standard Battle on the same map. This can confuse players a lot the first time they try it, a many of their favourite positions for Assault and Standard Battle just don't work properly on the new mode.

Encounter's single point is much slower to capture than those in Standard Battle. This, coupled with the fact that it is so exposed in the centre of the map, means that fast tanks breaking through the lines and quickly capturing the point is unlikely. Instead the match becomes a war of attrition, with actually capturing the point only viable once the majority of the other team are dealt with.

Simply rushing straight for the capture point is a foolish plan, however. Alternatively, you'll be wanting to look for a strong defensible position that overlooks the capture point. Most Encounter maps have this, the most famous being Himmelsdorf's huge hill (see First Battle Roll Out, page 28). While this hill is only worth it for the fastest of tanks in a standard battle, in Encounter it becomes crucial. Whoever wins the hill, wins the game. Most Encounter games will similarly be dominated by a single decisive fight.

TACTICS BY MAP

MALINOVKA

Malinovka is known as "campinovka" amongst the community due to most beginners simply sitting at either end and waiting for an opponent to make a mistake. Despite this, the key to the map is being proactive. By sending a wolfpack to conquer the hill and using aggressive scouting positions you can easily defeat a more stationary force.

1. Newbie tanks typically form up on these two lines and wait for one another to make a mistake. It is useful to have some heavy tanks or tank destroyers here, but not the entire team.

2. Charging right across this field results in instant death.

3. Medium tanks should be looking to seize this hill, allowing them to flank the enemy.

4. Light tanks can flank here, hiding in bushes to get good sightlines on the enemy.

5. More ambitious scouts can flank here, using the terrain slope to shield themselves from view. Just don't expose yourself by firing.

KARELIA

Karelia consists of a vulnerable centre ground with little cover and swamps that slow tanks down, flanked by two unusual rock formations that create intriguing battles. Artillery is dominant on this map, and is vital to support all assaults. Meanwhile, most of the fighting will take place on the flanks, among the rock formations and the famous "donut".

1. Heavy tanks should be playing peek-a-boom here, with slower mediums in support.

2. The faster tanks should flank along these lines.

3. When fighting the famous "donut" be sure to aim for the top end, not the bottom.

4. Artillery are very strong on Karelia, able to hit many exposed locations from their starting position.

5. For the gamblers amongst you, once the enemy has separated along the flanks a very fast light tank can dash up the middle and harass

ENSK

Ensk is a small map that features lots of close quarters fighting. The best tactics here are to push forward quickly and aggressively, pinning the enemy back and stopping them from taking up the good defensive positions.

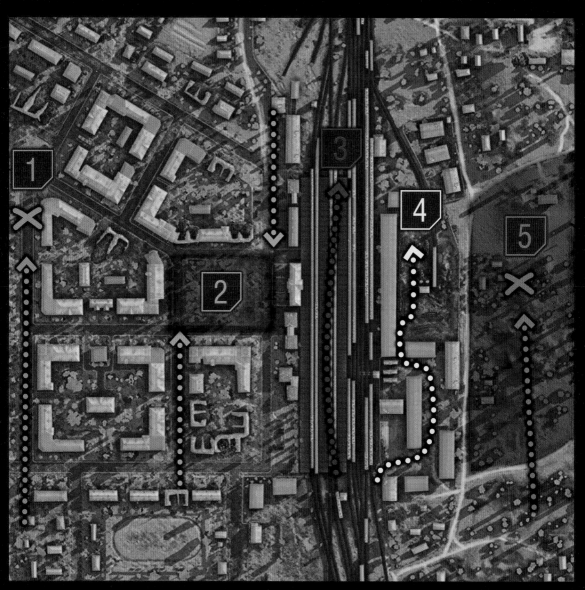

1. This line of attack is tempting, but very exposed. Make sure you guard it, but don't advance here.

2. The town square is where a lot of the most ferocious fighting on this map will take place. It is vital to defend it.

3. Using the train tracks will let you advance extremely quickly, but you will likely be spotted. Wait until everyone is focused on fighting before using it to launch a fast flanking attack.

4. These alleys provide excellent cover and the ability to flank enemies. Send a strong force here while the rest of the team occupies the town square.

5. The field is a death sentence to all but the fastest tanks.

EL HALLUF

El Halluf's signature feature is a deep valley in the centre, with very high cliffs around the edge. The valley is easy to get into, but hard to get out of, so much of the game revolves around changing elevation at the right time.

1. Most people's first inclination in El Hlaluf is to camp near these sniper spots. They're strong positions, but there's a lot more to the game than that.

2. Fast tanks should be taking this roundabout route to the southwest. Note that you could reach your destination faster by turning left before reaching the rocks, but you'd be less safe.

3. Most tanks that aren't extremely slow or extremely fast will head north.

4. The majority of the fighting will happen in this area.

LAKEVILLE

Lakeville is an unusual map in that anyone attacking the valley section is almost completely isolated from the rest of the game. Tanks taking the long central road and the city fight support each other, engaging in sniper crossfires to try and cause a breakthrough. One distinctive feature is the "cubby hole", a small kink in the road that allows aggressive scouts to hide away from the main battle.

1. The city lends itself towards heavy tank fighting. If you have a surplus of heavy tanks you'll want to push here.

2. This spot serves as a strong position for tanks in the city to snipe at tanks on the road.

3. More mobile tanks will push down the valley here, shielded from attack by the rock formations.

4. This corner serves as an excellent sniper position if paired with spotters in the city and the 'cubby hole'.

5. The small kink in the corner here is known as the "cubby hole". A fast scout can quickly get there and stay protected while spotting for snipers. This is easier if you're attacking from the north.

SIEGFRIED LINE

Another map built around an open field on one side and a crowded city on another. The key to Siegfried Line is realizing the east side of the city is surprisingly open and perfect for flanking attacks.

1. Rushing across the field is certain death until most of the enemies have been cleared.

2. Definitely occupy these defensive spots, which let you shoot down anyone attempting to cross the field. Then move up in the late game when most of the threats are gone.

3. Another city section that favours heavy tanks and close quarters fighting.

4. The east side of the town is surprisingly open, letting faster tanks quickly flank the city fighters and tip the balance of the game.

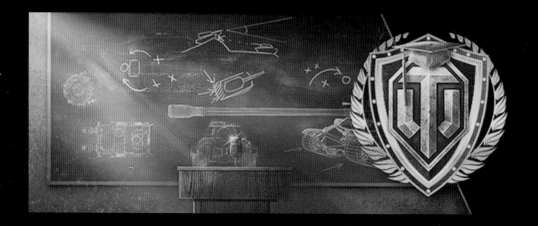

ADVANCED TACTICS

As you progress through World of Tanks, the basic skills you pick up will become perfected the more you play. However, getting from Tier V to X isn't as simple as a stroll in the park. Here is a selection of some of my favourite advanced tactics to keep you ticking along in one piece.

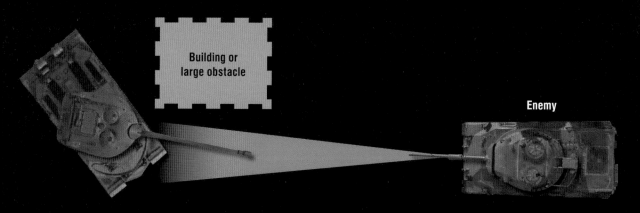

Building or large obstacle

Enemy

PEEK-A-BOOM

I've already touched on "peek-a-boom" several times in this section, but here's a more thorough explanation. Despite the heavy armour of tanks, they can always benefit from cover. Yet you'll want to get out from behind that cover to fire. Hence "peek-a-boom", where a tank carefully positions itself so it can edge out of cover to fire a shot, and back in to reload.

The strength of peek-a-boom is that it is easy to learn, but harder to perfect. Part of it is simply learning the rhythm of your tank, knowing when you are nearly ready to fire so

that you can spend as little time as possible out in the open. Part of it is the mind games that take place when two tanks are playing peek-a-boom together, each trying to get a moment where they can fire while their opponent cannot. There's also a positioning aspect, ideally you want to move out at an angle to best benefit from armour angling (see page 91). It's also best to use sniper mode as you edge out, as you can then instantly spot when your turret has a clear line of sight and stop.

CAROUSEL

Another tactic I've touched on before. The carousel is essentially the lost art of FPS circle strafing as applied to armoured warfare. It is the best way for a smaller, faster tank to attack an larger, heavier tank one on one. The trick is to not charge directly at the enemy but past it, turning in a tight circle around them, striking the rear and side armour while moving too quickly for the enemy tank's turret to track you.

This obviously works best with a fast tank with good turning and a fast firing gun. It is also wise to use the auto-aim ability (found by right clicking on a target) while doing this, as it will lock the turret to the enemy allowing you to concentrate on driving. Carousel tactics are usually done at short range, so you shouldn't have to worry much about inaccuracy, just keep firing.

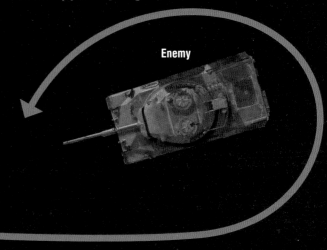

Enemy

SIDESCRAPING

Sidescraping is an alternative to "peek a boom". Instead of popping in and out of cover, you deliberately angle yourself so that only a slim portion of your side armour is exposed at an extreme angle, while you can fire back with impunity. You can get into position for a sidescrape by driving directly up to an obstacle so that the front of your tank is right up against it, then reversing away while turning slightly so that the rear of your tank sticks out. While this is happening, you should point your turret directly forward, stopping as soon as you have a clear view past the obstacle.

The result should be that only a small sliver of your side armour is visible, but at such an angle that you can bounce shells extremely well, while you have a clear view beyond your cover. Unlike a peek-a-boom you will usually stay stationary rather than popping in and out of cover, making you vulnerable to artillery and HE rounds, but extremely resistant to AP rounds, and capable of firing constantly. For obvious reasons this tactic shouldn't be used on tanks with weak side armour. It often works well on German heavy tanks, which suffer a collective weakness on the underside slope of their armour.

Building or large obstacle

Enemy

FACEHUGGING

Facehugging is a cuddly name for a not-so-cuddly tactic: namely driving directly at your opponent and engaging them at point blank range! This is actually far smarter than it sounds. The frontal armour on any tank is typically the strongest, so by getting right up close to an opponent you force them to hit you where it hurts least.

This strategy obviously works best with extremely well armoured tanks, mostly heavy tanks and late game tank destroyers. It works best with larger tanks with good gun depression, as they can use this to fire directly downwards into their enemy's fragile upper armour.

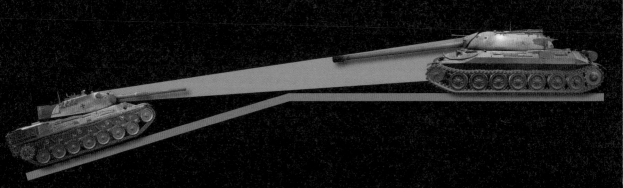

HULL DOWN

Hull down is a special technique where a tank positions itself part way up a hill with its gun angled downwards. The hull of the tank should be mostly or completely concealed by the hill, with only the turret and gun poking out above it. This makes the tank a much smaller target, and protects the hull from fire, with only the turret able to be hit. Good hull down tanks typically sport well armoured turrets and good "gun depression" (the ability to point their gun downwards), the latter ensures it can be pointed straight ahead why the tank itself is angled upward.

There are some drawbacks to going hull down. One is that it requires your tank to stay still in a very precise position, so it has no benefit if the enemy simply flanks you and attacks from behind, or drops an artillery round on you from above. The other is that if you push too far up the hill you will expose your underside to the enemy tank, having exactly the opposite effect. American tanks are the best at hull down tactics, as they typically have excellent gun depression and well armoured turrets.

ARMOUR ANGLING

As explained earlier, the angle at which a round strikes a tank's armour is crucial in World of Tanks. Armour is far easier to defeat if struck head on. Correctly angled armour is effectively much thicker to penetrate, and more likely to deflect shots. This effect can be amplified by positioning your tank carefully to control the angle of impact.

The key to this strategy is to never point your tank directly at your enemy. Instead you should point it at around 45%, then turn your turret to face ahead. It seems complicated, but you don't need to hit an exact angle, just making sure that you're slightly slanted will give you a big advantage. Russian tanks are particularly good at taking advantage of armour angling.

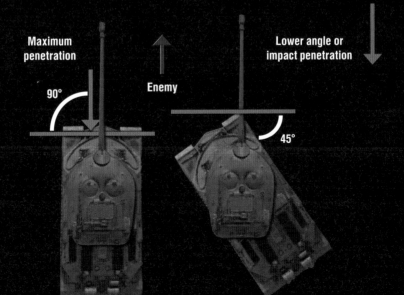

Maximum penetration

90°

Enemy

Lower angle or impact penetration

45°

SHOOT AND SCOOT

One of the most important things to learn in World of Tanks is when to move and when to stand still. A moving target is harder to hit, but tanks that are on the move are far less accurate and easier to spot. If you have a secure position to fire from, this isn't a problem, but if you need to cross open ground you need to "shoot and scoot". Broadly speaking, this means that you should move, stop, wait to aim, fire and then move again while reloading.

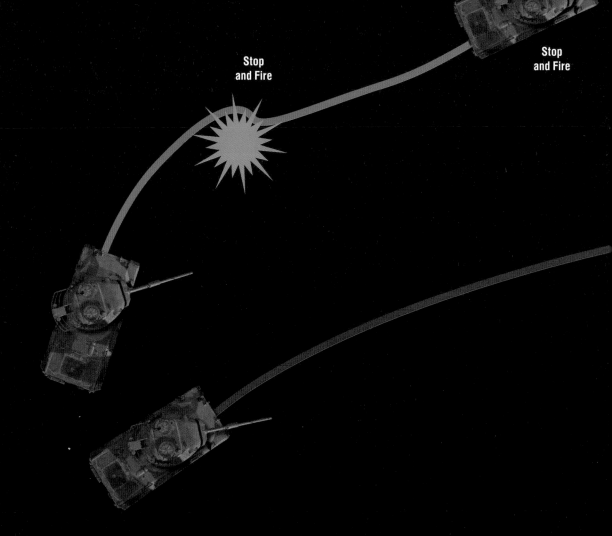

Stop
and Fire

Stop
and Fire

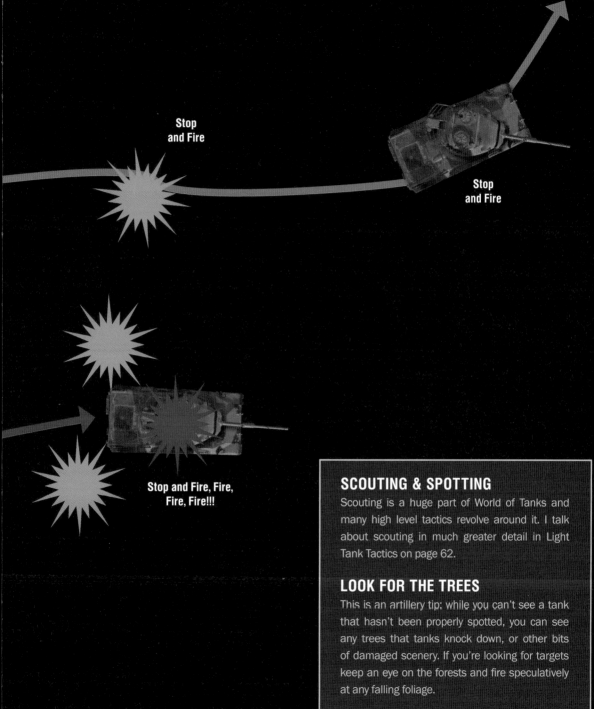

Stop
and Fire

Stop
and Fire

Stop and Fire, Fire,
Fire, Fire!!!

SCOUTING & SPOTTING

Scouting is a huge part of World of Tanks and many high level tactics revolve around it. I talk about scouting in much greater detail in Light Tank Tactics on page 62.

LOOK FOR THE TREES

This is an artillery tip; while you can't see a tank that hasn't been properly spotted, you can see any trees that tanks knock down, or other bits of damaged scenery. If you're looking for targets keep an eye on the forests and fire speculatively at any falling foliage.

HUG THE EDGE

Where possible, avoid taking wide corners in World of Tanks. Where possible, stick close to the edge and make a tight turn, exposing yourself as little as possible. This keeps half your side armour protected by the corner itself and makes you likely to present angled front armour to anyone lurking the other side of the corner. Just make sure you do it on an impenetrable obstacle, not a wall someone else can drive right through.

AIM FOR WEAKSPOTS

Every tank has points where its armour is weaker than others. You can find these by using the penetration indicator on the targeting reticule as explained on page 56. Weakspots are generally found where the hull is not smooth, hatches and mounted machine guns are perfect indicators of weak armour. You should pass your reticule over these before any other part of the tank, it will save you vital seconds.

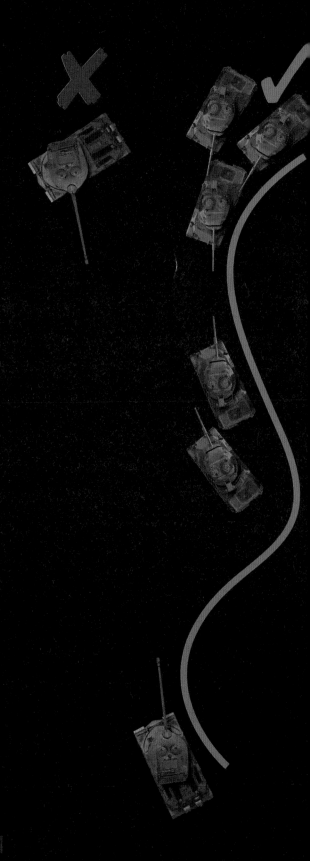

LEAD THE TARGET

World of Tanks' aiming system is a little unusual. Your shells drop with gravity over distance, but the aiming reticule compensates for that, so you don't need to compensate with your vertical aiming. Horizontally aiming, however, is a different matter: the reticule doesn't account for the speed a target is moving, so you'll have to learn to aim slightly ahead of it in order to make a decent impact.

STOP

SLOW

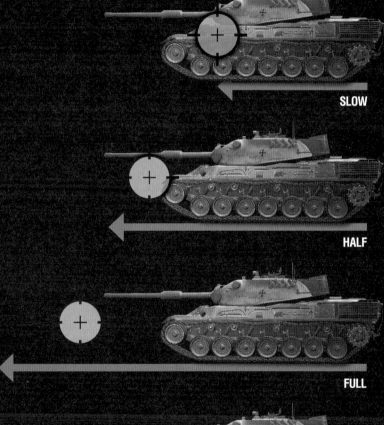

HALF

FULL

HAULING ASS!

PLATOONING

In the lower tiers of World of Tanks, most battles are very much "every tank for itself". Teams are as disorganized and chaotic as any other shooter. By creating a platoon (a two or three player group) and working together you can strike an advantage over the rest of the battlefield. What follows are a series of tips and teamwork tactics for playing together as a platoon. Almost all of the tips will also work without physically being in a platoon, but it's far easier to organize a group of three friends than a whole team of strangers!

ALWAYS USE VOICE CHAT

The first thing to remember when platooning is to always be on voice chat with your platoon. I don't care how fast your fingers are, nothing can replace the immediacy of talking. You can do this via the in-game voice chat or you can use an external client like Mumble or Teamspeak, both work well. The important part is being able to quickly make calls and immediately refer to something on the map without confusion.

Enemy

CO-OP COVER

This tactic involves one player picking a tough heavy tank or heavily armoured tank destroyer and providing a moving shield for one or two players with lighter armour and bigger guns. Like most tactics on this list, this can be performed without a platoon, it just works much better with one as the two players can properly co-ordinate and sync up, and the rear tank need not worry that their "cover'" will suddenly drive off and leave them exposed to enemy fire.

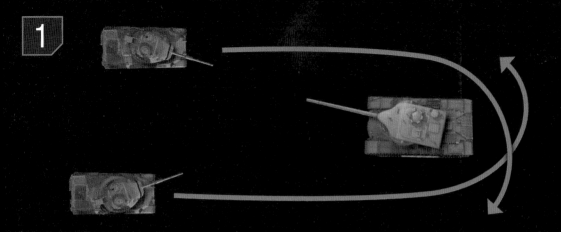

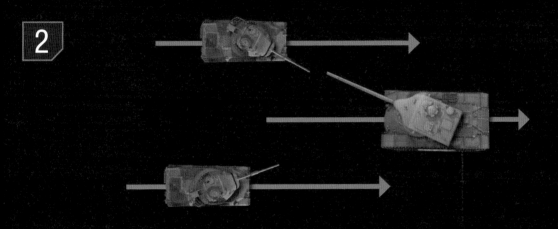

CROSSFIRE

A very basic pincer attack: two platoon-mates approach an enemy from opposite sides, forcing them to engage and turn their back on the other. This works even better in World of Tanks than regular first person shooters as tanks are limited by turret traverse speed, meaning they cannot turn quickly between the two enemies. The diagram above explains how to counter such a tactic: simply throw your tank into reverse until both the enemy tanks are forced to attack your front armour.

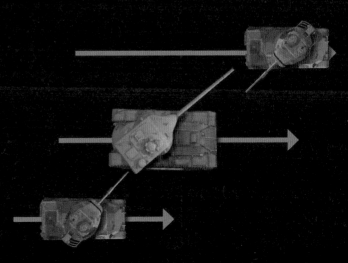

MANUAL SPOTTING

Another useful platoon tactic is for one player to take control of a scout tank while the other works as artillery. This allows you a bit more control over the usual spot-and-bombard tactics; the scout is able to deliberately call down fire rather than spotting and hoping. More importantly, it allows you to manually spot enemies. Sometimes a scout will spot an enemy, but will not be in radio range to relay that spot to the artillery, but if they're on voice chat with an artillery player they can ping the map and call for fire. Similarly, if they see an enemy vanish from view they can make an educated guess as to their location and call down fire upon it. You can do all these things without platooning of course, but your friend is more likely to listen to your guesses, and more likely to forgive you if they prove wrong!

BAIT

One of the most effective and risky moves a platoon can pull is for one platoon member to purposely lure the enemy into a trap. It's risky because whoever is playing 'bait' is going to purposely expose themselves to fire. Usually this will be a fast tank so they can quickly get away from trouble after getting the enemy to chase them, but it's wise to have a plan B if they get tracked.

A simple version of this is to have a tank peek around a corner, see the enemy and then rapidly reverse. The enemy tank will hopefully follow them, eager to get a shot off, only to be hit by multiple hidden snipers when they round the corner. Ideally these will be partially concealed in bushes to make them harder to detect.

The same trick can be pulled using a hill. The "bait" tank simply peeks over the top of the hill, drawing the attention of the enemy tank, then rapidly reverses back down. Meanwhile hidden snipers hide behind the hill, nailing the enemy on the vulnerable underside of their tank as they crest the ridge.

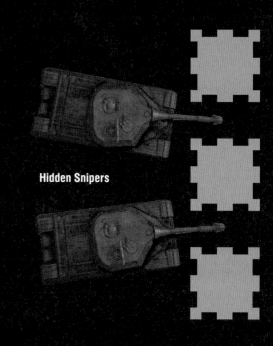

Hidden Snipers

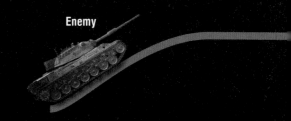

Enemy

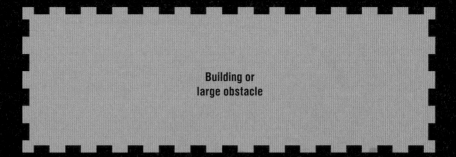

Building or
large obstacle

Enemy

Building or
large obstacle

Bait

Bait

Hidden Snipers

BRITISH TANK TREE

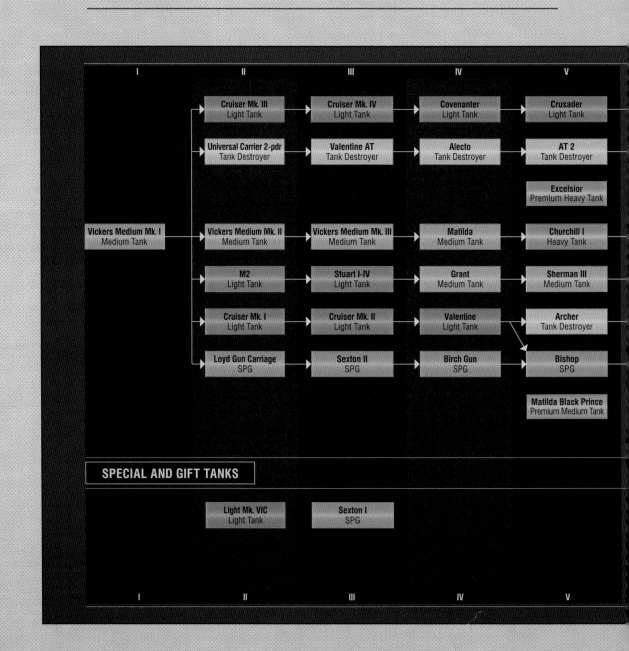

I	II	III	IV	V
	Cruiser Mk. III Light Tank	Cruiser Mk. IV Light Tank	Covenanter Light Tank	Crusader Light Tank
	Universal Carrier 2-pdr Tank Destroyer	Valentine AT Tank Destroyer	Alecto Tank Destroyer	AT 2 Tank Destroyer
				Excelsior Premium Heavy Tank
Vickers Medium Mk. I Medium Tank	Vickers Medium Mk. II Medium Tank	Vickers Medium Mk. III Medium Tank	Matilda Medium Tank	Churchill I Heavy Tank
	M2 Light Tank	Stuart I-IV Light Tank	Grant Medium Tank	Sherman III Medium Tank
	Cruiser Mk. I Light Tank	Cruiser Mk. II Light Tank	Valentine Light Tank	Archer Tank Destroyer
	Loyd Gun Carriage SPG	Sexton II SPG	Birch Gun SPG	Bishop SPG
				Matilda Black Prince Premium Medium Tank

SPECIAL AND GIFT TANKS

	Light Mk. VIC Light Tank	Sexton I SPG		

I	II	III	IV	V

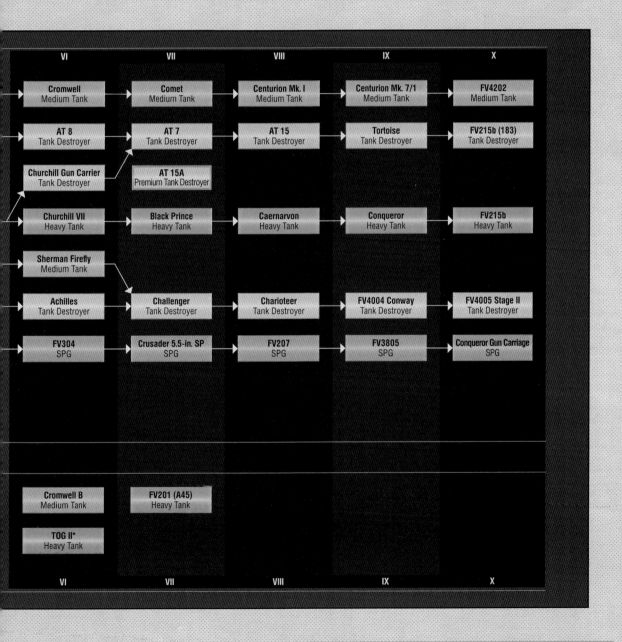

VI	VII	VIII	IX	X
Cromwell Medium Tank	**Comet** Medium Tank	**Centurion Mk. I** Medium Tank	**Centurion Mk. 7/1** Medium Tank	**FV4202** Medium Tank
AT 8 Tank Destroyer	**AT 7** Tank Destroyer	**AT 15** Tank Destroyer	**Tortoise** Tank Destroyer	**FV215b (183)** Tank Destroyer
Churchill Gun Carrier Tank Destroyer	**AT 15A** Premium Tank Destroyer			
Churchill VII Heavy Tank	**Black Prince** Heavy Tank	**Caernarvon** Heavy Tank	**Conqueror** Heavy Tank	**FV215b** Heavy Tank
Sherman Firefly Medium Tank				
Achilles Tank Destroyer	**Challenger** Tank Destroyer	**Charioteer** Tank Destroyer	**FV4004 Conway** Tank Destroyer	**FV4005 Stage II** Tank Destroyer
FV304 SPG	**Crusader 5.5-in. SP** SPG	**FV207** SPG	**FV3805** SPG	**Conqueror Gun Carriage** SPG
Cromwell B Medium Tank	**FV201 (A45)** Heavy Tank			
TOG II* Heavy Tank				

VI VII VIII IX X

CHINESE TANK TREE

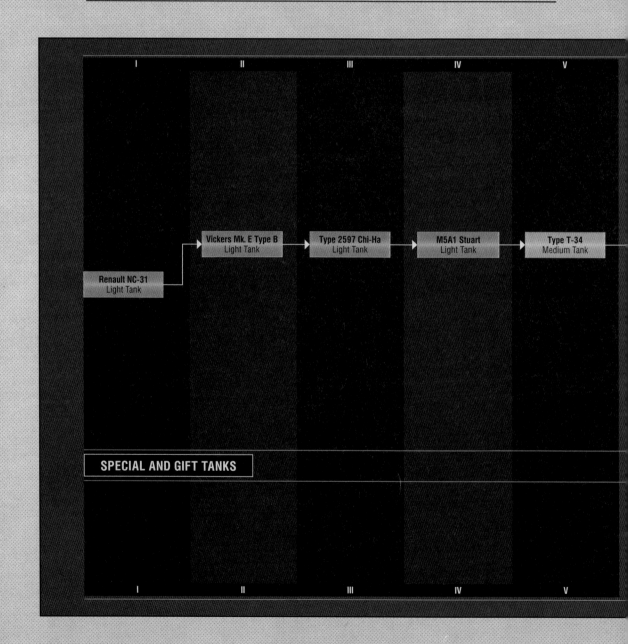

I	II	III	IV	V
	Vickers Mk. E Type B Light Tank	**Type 2597 Chi-Ha** Light Tank	**M5A1 Stuart** Light Tank	**Type T-34** Medium Tank
Renault NC-31 Light Tank				

SPECIAL AND GIFT TANKS

I	II	III	IV	V

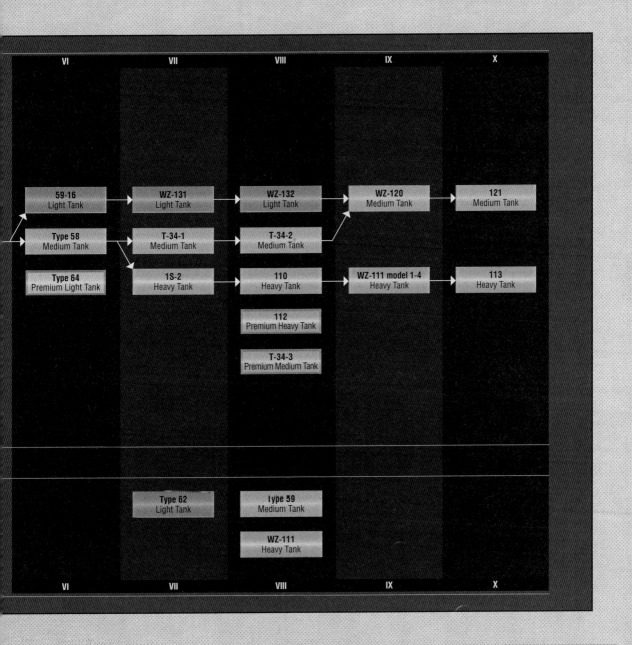

FRENCH TANK TREE

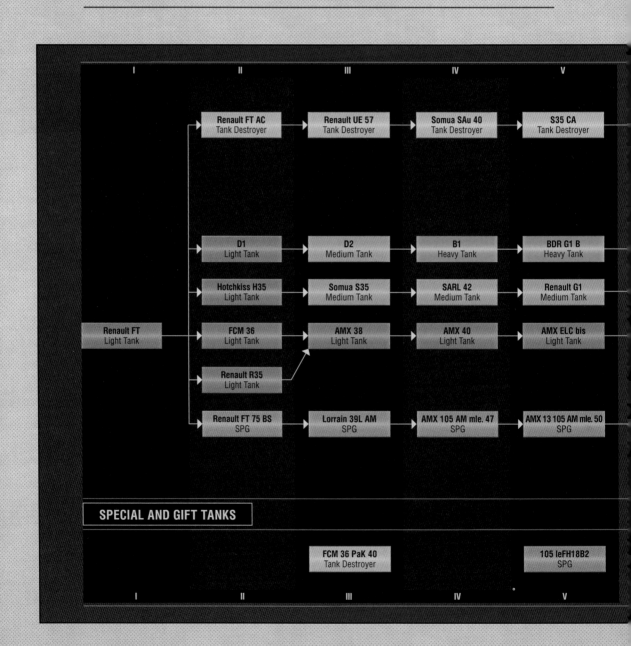

	I	II	III	IV	V
		Renault FT AC Tank Destroyer	**Renault UE 57** Tank Destroyer	**Somua SAu 40** Tank Destroyer	**S35 CA** Tank Destroyer
		D1 Light Tank	**D2** Medium Tank	**B1** Heavy Tank	**BDR G1 B** Heavy Tank
		Hotchkiss H35 Light Tank	**Somua S35** Medium Tank	**SARL 42** Medium Tank	**Renault G1** Medium Tank
	Renault FT Light Tank	**FCM 36** Light Tank	**AMX 38** Light Tank	**AMX 40** Light Tank	**AMX ELC bis** Light Tank
		Renault R35 Light Tank			
		Renault FT 75 BS SPG	**Lorrain 39L AM** SPG	**AMX 105 AM mle. 47** SPG	**AMX 13 105 AM mle. 50** SPG

SPECIAL AND GIFT TANKS

	I	II	III	IV	V
			FCM 36 PaK 40 Tank Destroyer		**105 leFH18B2** SPG

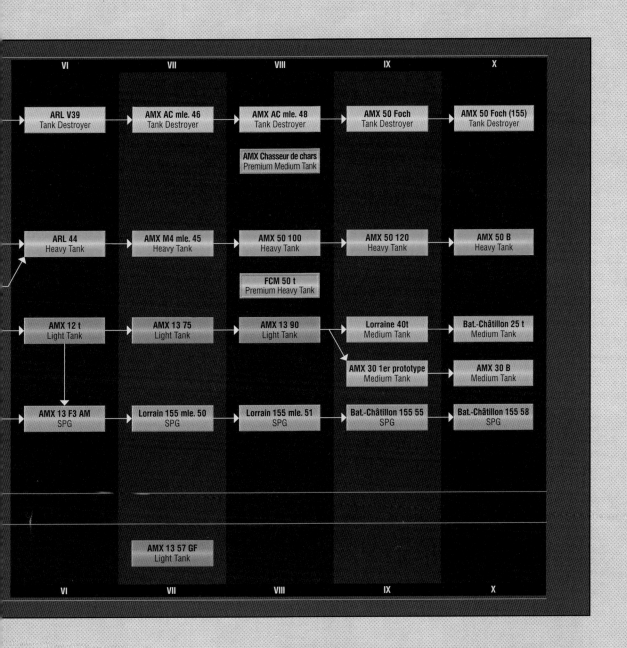

VI	VII	VIII	IX	X
ARL V39 Tank Destroyer	**AMX AC mle. 46** Tank Destroyer	**AMX AC mle. 48** Tank Destroyer	**AMX 50 Foch** Tank Destroyer	**AMX 50 Foch (155)** Tank Destroyer
		AMX Chasseur de chars Premium Medium Tank		
ARL 44 Heavy Tank	**AMX M4 mle. 45** Heavy Tank	**AMX 50 100** Heavy Tank	**AMX 50 120** Heavy Tank	**AMX 50 B** Heavy Tank
		FCM 50 t Premium Heavy Tank		
AMX 12 t Light Tank	**AMX 13 75** Light Tank	**AMX 13 90** Light Tank	**Lorraine 40t** Medium Tank	**Bat.-Châtillon 25 t** Medium Tank
			AMX 30 1er prototype Medium Tank	**AMX 30 B** Medium Tank
AMX 13 F3 AM SPG	**Lorrain 155 mle. 50** SPG	**Lorrain 155 mle. 51** SPG	**Bat.-Châtillon 155 55** SPG	**Bat.-Châtillon 155 58** SPG
	AMX 13 57 GF Light Tank			

GERMAN TANK TREE

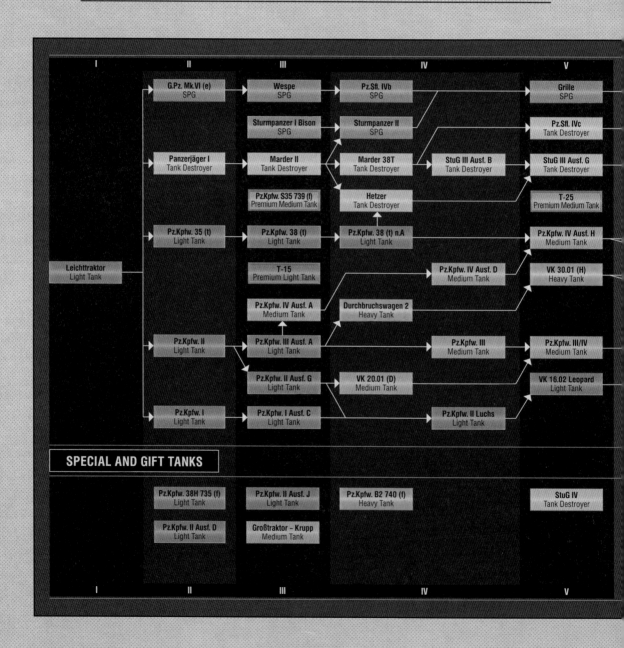

I	II	III	IV	V
	G.Pz. Mk.VI (e) SPG	**Wespe** SPG	**Pz.Sfl. IVb** SPG	**Grille** SPG
		Sturmpanzer I Bison SPG	**Sturmpanzer II** SPG	**Pz.Sfl. IVc** Tank Destroyer
	Panzerjäger I Tank Destroyer	**Marder II** Tank Destroyer	**Marder 38T** Tank Destroyer	**StuG III Ausf. B** Tank Destroyer	**StuG III Ausf. G** Tank Destroyer
		Pz.Kpfw. S35 739 (f) Premium Medium Tank	**Hetzer** Tank Destroyer		**T-25** Premium Medium Tank
	Pz.Kpfw. 35 (t) Light Tank	**Pz.Kpfw. 38 (t)** Light Tank	**Pz.Kpfw. 38 (t) n.A** Light Tank		**Pz.Kpfw. IV Ausf. H** Medium Tank
Leichttraktor Light Tank		**T-15** Premium Light Tank		**Pz.Kpfw. IV Ausf. D** Medium Tank	**VK 30.01 (H)** Heavy Tank
		Pz.Kpfw. IV Ausf. A Medium Tank	**Durchbruchswagen 2** Heavy Tank		
	Pz.Kpfw. II Light Tank	**Pz.Kpfw. III Ausf. A** Light Tank		**Pz.Kpfw. III** Medium Tank	**Pz.Kpfw. III/IV** Medium Tank
		Pz.Kpfw. II Ausf. G Light Tank	**VK 20.01 (D)** Medium Tank		**VK 16.02 Leopard** Light Tank
	Pz.Kpfw. I Light Tank	**Pz.Kpfw. I Ausf. C** Light Tank		**Pz.Kpfw. II Luchs** Light Tank	

SPECIAL AND GIFT TANKS

	II	III	IV	V
	Pz.Kpfw. 38H 735 (f) Light Tank	**Pz.Kpfw. II Ausf. J** Light Tank	**Pz.Kpfw. B2 740 (f)** Heavy Tank	**StuG IV** Tank Destroyer
	Pz.Kpfw. II Ausf. D Light Tank	**Großtraktor – Krupp** Medium Tank		

I	II	III	IV	V

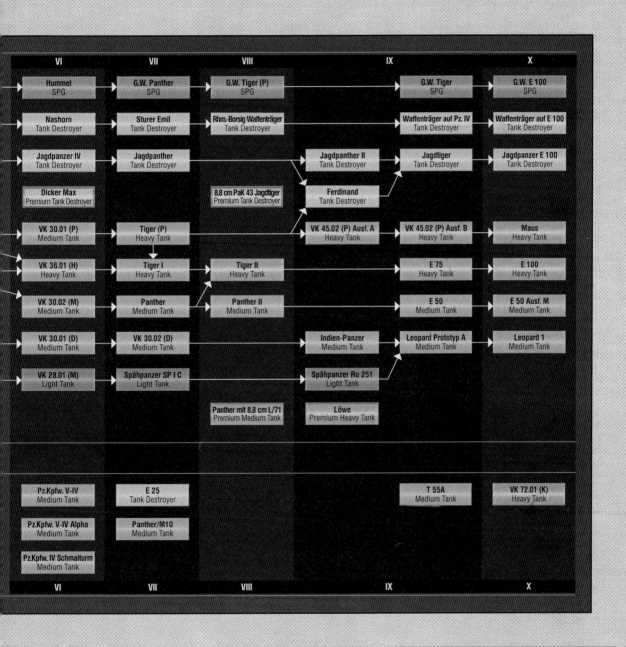

VI	VII	VIII	IX	X
Hummel SPG	**G.W. Panther** SPG	**G.W. Tiger (P)** SPG	**G.W. Tiger** SPG	**G.W. E 100** SPG
Nashorn Tank Destroyer	**Sturer Emil** Tank Destroyer	**Rhm.-Borsig Waffenträger** Tank Destroyer	**Waffenträger auf Pz. IV** Tank Destroyer	**Waffenträger auf E 100** Tank Destroyer
Jagdpanzer IV Tank Destroyer	**Jagdpanther** Tank Destroyer	**Jagdpanther II** Tank Destroyer	**Jagdtiger** Tank Destroyer	**Jagdpanzer E 100** Tank Destroyer
Dicker Max Premium Tank Destroyer		**8,8 cm PaK 43 Jagdtiger** Premium Tank Destroyer	**Ferdinand** Tank Destroyer	
VK 30.01 (P) Medium Tank	**Tiger (P)** Heavy Tank		**VK 45.02 (P) Ausf. A** Heavy Tank	**VK 45.02 (P) Ausf. B** Heavy Tank	**Maus** Heavy Tank
VK 36.01 (H) Heavy Tank	**Tiger I** Heavy Tank	**Tiger II** Heavy Tank	**E 75** Heavy Tank	**E 100** Heavy Tank
VK 30.02 (M) Medium Tank	**Panther** Medium Tank	**Panther II** Medium Tank	**E 50** Medium Tank	**E 50 Ausf. M** Medium Tank
VK 30.01 (D) Medium Tank	**VK 30.02 (D)** Medium Tank	**Indien-Panzer** Medium Tank	**Leopard Prototyp A** Medium Tank	**Leopard 1** Medium Tank
VK 28.01 (M) Light Tank	**Spähpanzer SP I C** Light Tank	**Spähpanzer Ru 251** Light Tank		
		Panther mit 8,8 cm L/71 Premium Medium Tank	**Löwe** Premium Heavy Tank	
Pz.Kpfw. V-IV Medium Tank	**E 25** Tank Destroyer		**T 55A** Medium Tank	**VK 72.01 (K)** Heavy Tank
Pz.Kpfw. V-IV Alpha Medium Tank	**Panther/M10** Medium Tank			
Pz.Kpfw. IV Schmalturm Medium Tank				

| VI | VII | VIII | IX | X |

JAPANESE TANK TREE

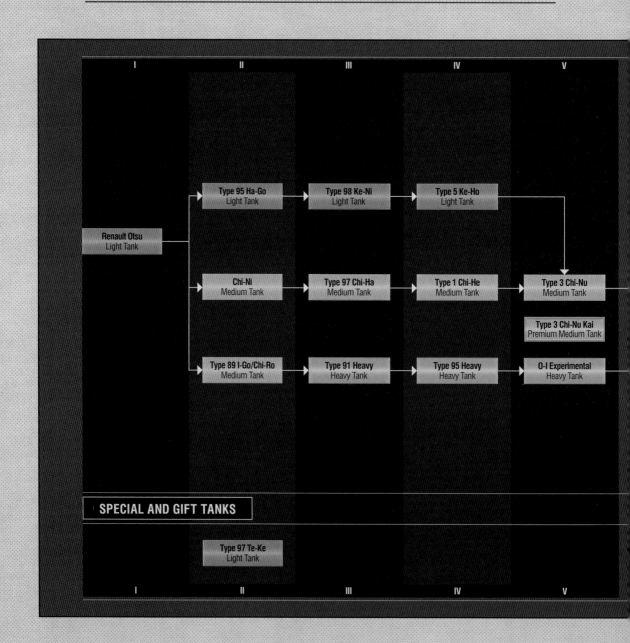

	I	II	III	IV	V
		Type 95 Ha-Go Light Tank	Type 98 Ke-Ni Light Tank	Type 5 Ke-Ho Light Tank	
	Renault Otsu Light Tank	Chi-Ni Medium Tank	Type 97 Chi-Ha Medium Tank	Type 1 Chi-He Medium Tank	Type 3 Chi-Nu Medium Tank
					Type 3 Chi-Nu Kai Premium Medium Tank
		Type 89 I-Go/Chi-Ro Medium Tank	Type 91 Heavy Heavy Tank	Type 95 Heavy Heavy Tank	O-I Experimental Heavy Tank

SPECIAL AND GIFT TANKS

		Type 97 Te-Ke Light Tank			

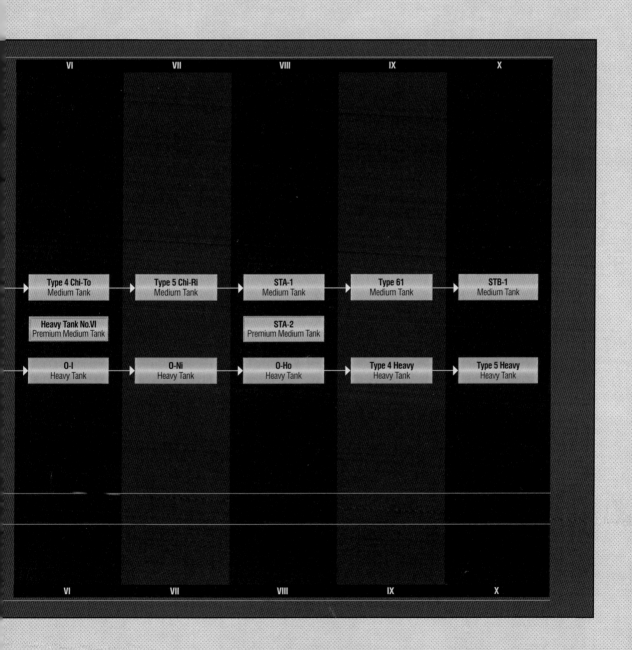

SOVIET TANK TREE

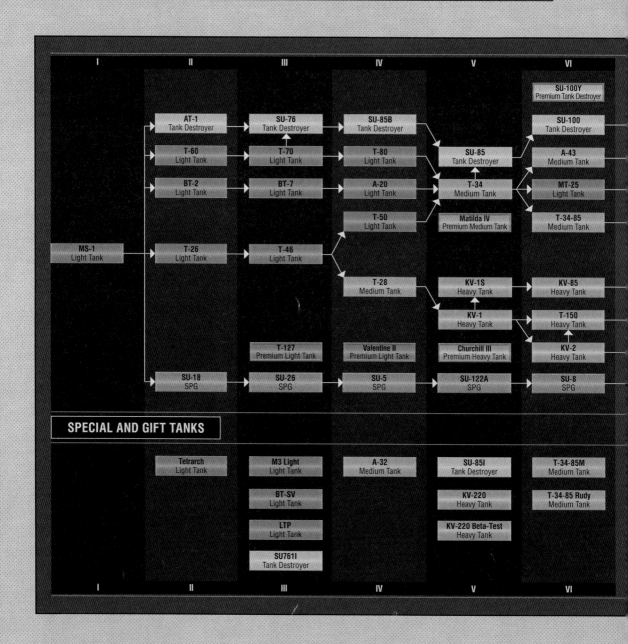

	I	II	III	IV	V	VI
						SU-100Y Premium Tank Destroyer
		AT-1 Tank Destroyer	**SU-76** Tank Destroyer	**SU-85B** Tank Destroyer		**SU-100** Tank Destroyer
		T-60 Light Tank	**T-70** Light Tank	**T-80** Light Tank	**SU-85** Tank Destroyer	**A-43** Medium Tank
		BT-2 Light Tank	**BT-7** Light Tank	**A-20** Light Tank	**T-34** Medium Tank	**MT-25** Light Tank
				T-50 Light Tank	**Matilda IV** Premium Medium Tank	**T-34-85** Medium Tank
	MS-1 Light Tank	**T-26** Light Tank	**T-46** Light Tank			
				T-28 Medium Tank	**KV-1S** Heavy Tank	**KV-85** Heavy Tank
					KV-1 Heavy Tank	**T-150** Heavy Tank
			T-127 Premium Light Tank	**Valentine II** Premium Light Tank	**Churchill III** Premium Heavy Tank	**KV-2** Heavy Tank
		SU-18 SPG	**SU-26** SPG	**SU-5** SPG	**SU-122A** SPG	**SU-8** SPG

SPECIAL AND GIFT TANKS

I	II	III	IV	V	VI
	Tetrarch Light Tank	**M3 Light** Light Tank	**A-32** Medium Tank	**SU-85I** Tank Destroyer	**T-34-85M** Medium Tank
		BT-SV Light Tank		**KV-220** Heavy Tank	**T-34-85 Rudy** Medium Tank
		LTP Light Tank		**KV-220 Beta-Test** Heavy Tank	
		SU761I Tank Destroyer			

| I | II | III | IV | V | VI |

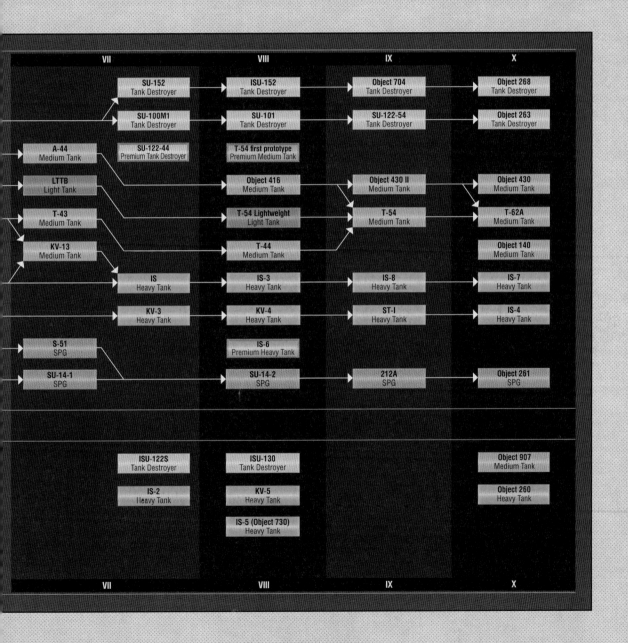

VII	VIII	IX	X
SU-152 Tank Destroyer	**ISU-152** Tank Destroyer	**Object 704** Tank Destroyer	**Object 268** Tank Destroyer
SU-100M1 Tank Destroyer	**SU-101** Tank Destroyer	**SU-122-54** Tank Destroyer	**Object 263** Tank Destroyer
A-44 Medium Tank / **SU-122-44** Premium Tank Destroyer	**T-54 first prototype** Premium Medium Tank		
LTTB Light Tank	**Object 416** Medium Tank	**Object 430 II** Medium Tank	**Object 430** Medium Tank
T-43 Medium Tank	**T-54 Lightweight** Light Tank	**T-54** Medium Tank	**T-62A** Medium Tank
KV-13 Medium Tank	**T-44** Medium Tank		**Object 140** Medium Tank
IS Heavy Tank	**IS-3** Heavy Tank	**IS-8** Heavy Tank	**IS-7** Heavy Tank
KV-3 Heavy Tank	**KV-4** Heavy Tank	**ST-I** Heavy Tank	**IS-4** Heavy Tank
S-51 SPG	**IS-6** Premium Heavy Tank		
SU-14-1 SPG	**SU-14-2** SPG	**212A** SPG	**Object 261** SPG
ISU-122S Tank Destroyer	**ISU-130** Tank Destroyer		**Object 907** Medium Tank
IS-2 Heavy Tank	**KV-5** Heavy Tank		**Object 260** Heavy Tank
	IS-5 (Object 730) Heavy Tank		

AMERICAN TANK TREE

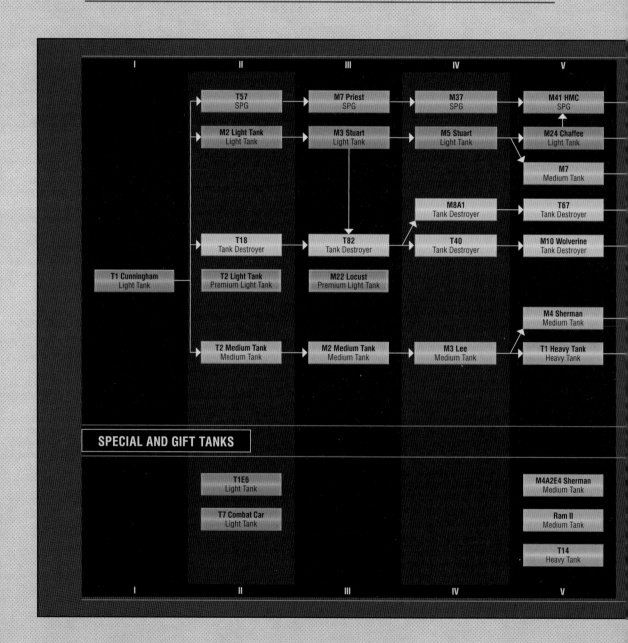

	I	II	III	IV	V
SPG		T57 SPG	M7 Priest SPG	M37 SPG	M41 HMC SPG
Light Tank		M2 Light Tank Light Tank	M3 Stuart Light Tank	M5 Stuart Light Tank	M24 Chaffee Light Tank
Medium Tank					M7 Medium Tank
Tank Destroyer				M8A1 Tank Destroyer	T67 Tank Destroyer
Tank Destroyer		T18 Tank Destroyer	T82 Tank Destroyer	T40 Tank Destroyer	M10 Wolverine Tank Destroyer
Light Tank	T1 Cunningham Light Tank	T2 Light Tank Premium Light Tank	M22 Locust Premium Light Tank		
Medium Tank					M4 Sherman Medium Tank
Medium Tank		T2 Medium Tank Medium Tank	M2 Medium Tank Medium Tank	M3 Lee Medium Tank	T1 Heavy Tank Heavy Tank

SPECIAL AND GIFT TANKS

	I	II	III	IV	V
		T1E6 Light Tank			M4A2E4 Sherman Medium Tank
		T7 Combat Car Light Tank			Ram II Medium Tank
					T14 Heavy Tank

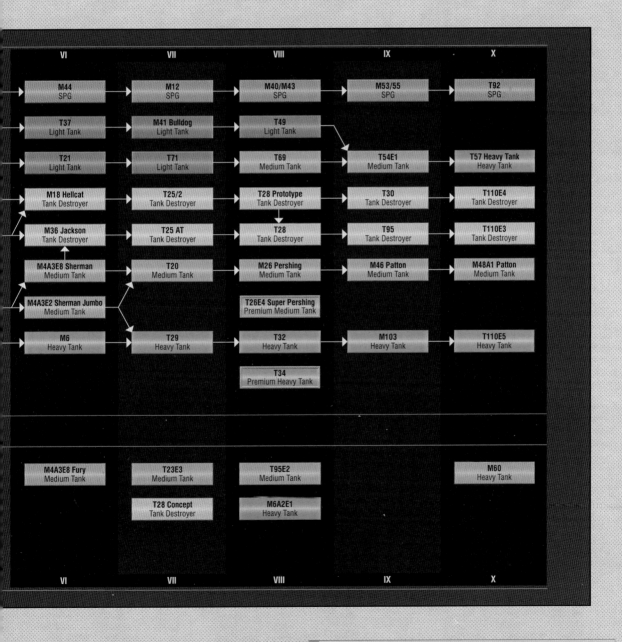

VI	VII	VIII	IX	X
M44 SPG	**M12** SPG	**M40/M43** SPG	**M53/55** SPG	**T92** SPG
T37 Light Tank	**M41 Bulldog** Light Tank	**T49** Light Tank		
T21 Light Tank	**T71** Light Tank	**T69** Medium Tank	**T54E1** Medium Tank	**T57 Heavy Tank** Heavy Tank
M18 Hellcat Tank Destroyer	**T25/2** Tank Destroyer	**T28 Prototype** Tank Destroyer	**T30** Tank Destroyer	**T110E4** Tank Destroyer
M36 Jackson Tank Destroyer	**T25 AT** Tank Destroyer	**T28** Tank Destroyer	**T95** Tank Destroyer	**T110E3** Tank Destroyer
M4A3E8 Sherman Medium Tank	**T20** Medium Tank	**M26 Pershing** Medium Tank	**M46 Patton** Medium Tank	**M48A1 Patton** Medium Tank
M4A3E2 Sherman Jumbo Medium Tank		**T26E4 Super Pershing** Premium Medium Tank		
M6 Heavy Tank	**T29** Heavy Tank	**T32** Heavy Tank	**M103** Heavy Tank	**T110E5** Heavy Tank
		T34 Premium Heavy Tank		

VI	VII	VIII	IX	X
M4A3E8 Fury Medium Tank	**T23E3** Medium Tank	**T95E2** Medium Tank		**M60** Heavy Tank
	T28 Concept Tank Destroyer	**M6A2E1** Heavy Tank		

ACHIEVEMENTS

MEDALS AND RIBBONS

Winning medals and ribbons can be a satisfying end to an epic battle in which you had excelled. Some of these are easier to obtain than others, and this section lists what you will have to do to earn the recognition of your peers!

MASTERY BADGES

MASTERY BADGE III CLASS
Earn more experience in a single battle than the average highest experience of 50% of all players in the same tank within the last seven days.

MASTERY BADGE II CLASS
Earn more experience in a single battle than the average highest experience of 80% of all players in the same tank within the last seven days.

MASTERY BADGE I CLASS
Earn more experience in a single battle than the average highest experience of 95% of all players in the same tank within the last seven days.

MASTERY BADGE ACE TANKER
Earn more experience in a single battle than the average highest experience of 99% of all players in the same tank within the last seven days.

BATTLE ACHIEVEMENTS

TOP GUN
Destroy at least six enemy vehicles during the battle.

If two or more players tie for the most number of destroyed vehicles (at least six) the achievement is granted to the player that earned the most XP.

SNIPER
With the release of Version 0.8.11, this medal is no longer being awarded. Prior to 0.8.11, this was awarded when you achieved at least 85% hits out of a minimum of ten shots fired with the potential damage of 1,000 HP and more. Non-penetrating hits are included, but hits on friendly units are not included.

If two or more players have an equal hit ratio, the achievement is granted to the player with the highest potential damage. If two or more players have an equal amount of potential damage, the achievement is granted to the player who earned more XP for the battle, including additional XP provided to Premium Account users. If the amount of XP is equal as well, the achievement is not granted.

INVADER
Capture the maximum number of points from the enemy base, a total no less than 80.

The achievement is granted on successful base capture, including only the points that were part of the base capture. If the battle ends in a draw, the achievement is granted to the first player to receive 80 or more capture points.

TANK SNIPER
Awarded to a player who has, during the battle, dealt the largest amount of damage from a distance of at least 300 meters with at least eight accurate shots. At least 80% of the total hits must inflict damage or be a critical hit. The overall accuracy must be at least

85%. The damage dealt must exceed the amount of the player's tank's HP and be at least 1,000. To receive this award, allies must not be hit with any direct shots. If two or more players have dealt an equal amount of damage, the achievement is granted to the player that earned more XP. Can be obtained in Random Battles only.

HIGH CALIBRE
Awarded to players who wreak the highest amount of damage during the battle. The damage dealt should be at least 20% of enemy team tanks' HP sum, and greater than 1,000 points. To receive this award, the player must not hit any allies by direct shot. If two or more players deal an equal amount of damage, and also qualify for High Calibre, the achievement is granted to whichever player earned more XP.

DEFENDER
Reduce the amount of enemy capture points on a friendly base by 70 or more.
If two or more players have reduced equal amount of capture points, the achievement is granted to whichever player earned more XP.

STEEL WALL
Receive the most hits (at least 11) of any player on your team, with potential damage of at least 1,000 HP, and survive.
If two players qualify for the award, the player with the highest potential damage gets Steel Wall. If both players have the same potential damage, the player that took more hits is awarded the Steel Wall. If both players took the same amount of potential damage, XP is used to break the tie.

CONFEDERATE
Hit more enemy vehicles than any other player on your team (at least six), which are subsequently destroyed by another player.
If two or more players have equal amount of hits, the achievement is granted to the player that earned more EXP.

SCOUT
Be the first to detect nine or more enemy tanks and self-propelled guns. The achievement is granted to the winning team only.

PATROL DUTY
Awarded to the player who helps the team damage at least six enemy vehicles by highlighting them. The tanks must be highlighted only by you when they take damage. If two players gain the same amount of assistance damage this way, the award is given to the player that earned more EXP.

BROTHERS IN ARMS
Awarded to a platoon in which all platoon members destroy at least three enemy vehicles and survive in battle. Each participant receives this title.

CRUCIAL CONTRIBUTION
Awarded to a platoon which destroyed at least 12 enemy vehicles in one battle. Each platoon participant receive this title.

WOLF AMONG SHEEP
Awarded to a player who was the top player by damage inflicted in 100 battles. The awards are accumulative. Available in Team Battles only. This achievement was added in 0.9.0.

ARMOURED FIST
Awarded to all members of a team which has destroyed the whole enemy team with losing no more than one vehicle. Available only in Team Battle mode. This achievement was added in 0.9.0.

WAR GENIUS
Awarded to a player who has been the top player by experience earned in a total of 100 victorious battles. The total accumulates over time. Available in Team Battles only. This Achievement was added in 0.9.0.

COMMEMORATIVE ACHIEVEMENTS

COOL-HEADED
Survive at least ten ricochets and non-penetrations in a row from enemy players.

LUCKY
Witness the destruction of an enemy vehicle by an enemy team player. You must be within ten metres or less from the enemy vehicle at the moment of its destruction.

SPARTAN
Survive a ricochet or non-penetrating shot from an enemy player. Your vehicle must have less than 10% of its hit points (HP) left and you must survive.

RANGER
Destroy all enemy light tanks (at least three) in the course of one battle

GOD OF WAR
While driving a SPG, be the last survivor and win the battle. Available in Team Battles only.

KING OF THE HILL
Awarded to a player whose vehicle is the only one to have survived in the battle. In order to receive this achievement you must play on a tank or tank destroyer. Available in Team Battles only.

NO MAN'S LAND
End a battle in a draw where both teams are completely destroyed. Awarded to all members of both teams. Can be obtained in Team Battles only.

ROCK SOLID
While driving an SPG, destroy an enemy vehicle by ramming and survive. SPG's speed must be less than 10 km/h. The player must not destroy any allied vehicles. Can be obtained in Random Battles only.

EPIC ACHIEVEMENTS

BÖLTER'S MEDAL
With the release of Version 0.8.0, this medal is no longer being awarded. Prior to 0.8.0, this was awarded for destroying seven or more enemy tanks and self-propelled guns with a tank or tank destroyer, or ten or more vehicles with a self-propelled gun in one battle. The targets must be at least Tier IV enemy vehicles.

Johannes Bölter was one of the most successful German tank aces of World War II. He participated in operations in the invasions of Poland, France, Greece and the Soviet Union, and the defence of France.

BILLOTTE'S MEDAL
Awarded to players who destroy at least one enemy vehicle and survive the battle to victory despite receiving at least five different critical hits and 80% or more loss of hit points.

Pierre Billotte was a captain in the French Army who destroyed two PzKpfw IV, 11 PzKpfw III and two guns with his Char B1 on 16 May, 1940.

TARCZAY'S MEDAL
Awarded to players who destroy at least five enemy vehicles and survive the battle to victory despite receiving at least five different critical hits and 80% or more loss of hit points.

Ervin Tarczay was a Hungarian tank ace. He fought with the Hungarian 2nd Armoured Division and destroyed at least ten enemy vehicles.

ORLIK'S MEDAL
Awarded for destroying three or more enemy tanks or tank destroyers with a light tank. The targets must be at least two tiers higher than the player's tank.

Roman Edmund Orlik, a Polish Army sergeant, was a tank ace who knocked out 13 German tanks with his light TKS tankette in September, 1939.

HALONEN'S MEDAL

Awarded for destroying three or more enemy vehicles with a tank destroyer. The targets must be at least two tiers higher than the player's vehicle.

Erkki Halonen, a sergeant in the Finnish Army and a tank ace, destroyed three T-34, two KV-1, and two ISU-152 with his StuG III in battles during June and July, 1944.

FADIN'S MEDAL

Awarded for destroying the last enemy vehicle in the battle with the last shell remaining in the player's tank.

A hero of the Soviet Union, Alexander Fadin was a T-34 commander. Supported by one infantry platoon, Fadin managed to capture and hold the Dashukovka village for five hours with one tank, and destroyed three tanks, one halftrack, two mortars and 12 machine gun nests. His crew also shot down an enemy plane with his tank's coaxial machine gun.

TAMADA YOSHIO MEDAL
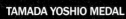
Awarded to a player who destroys at least three self-propelled Guns while driving a light tank, and survives the battle. The targets must be at least two tiers higher than the player's tank.

Tamada Yoshio commanded the Japanese 4th Tank Regiment (Type 95 Ha-Gō light tanks) in an attack that overran and destroyed twelve Russian artillery guns during the Second Sino-Japanese War in July 1939.

DE LANGLADE'S MEDAL
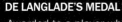
Awarded to a player who in the course of one battle destroys four enemy vehicles within a base circle while they are attempting to capture the base. Enemy vehicles may attempt to capture the base all at once or in turn.

On 13 September 1944, Colonel Paul Girot de Langlade's Groupement Tactique "Langlade" (G.T.L),

outnumbered by over two to one, attacked a German 112th Panzer Regiment occupying the French village of Dompaire. In the ensuing battle de Langlade's 16 M4A2 tanks and four M10 tank destroyers, with support from French artillery and American fighter-bombers, destroyed 69 of 90 PzKpfw V Panther and PzKpfw IV tanks.

RASEINIAI HEROES' MEDAL

Awarded to a player who destroys single-handedly all enemy vehicles (at least 14 vehicles).

In June 1941, near the Lithuanian town of Raseiniai, roughly 20 KV tanks of the Soviet 3rd Mechanized Corps met the assault of the 6th Panzer Division, with approximately 100 vehicles. A single KV-2 tank managed to hold off the German advance for a full day while being pummeled by a variety of antitank weapons, until finally the KV-2 ran out of ammunition and was knocked out.

POOL'S MEDAL

Awarded to players in vehicles of Tier V or higher for destroying 10–13 enemy vehicles in one battle.

Lafayette G. Pool is widely recognized as the U.S. tank ace of aces, credited with 12 confirmed tank kills and 258 total armoured vehicle and self-propelled gun kills.

NICOLS' MEDAL
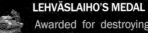
Awarded for destroying four or more enemy vehicles with a medium tank. The targets must be at least two tiers higher than the player's tank.

Alfie Nicols was a British tank gunner. During the battle of El Alamein he destroyed fourteen enemy vehicles.

LEHVÄSLAIHO'S MEDAL
Awarded for destroying two enemy vehicles with a medium tank. The targets must be at least two tiers higher than the player's tank.

Reino Lehväslaiho was a Finnish tank ace who destroyed seven tanks and tank destroyers.

OSKIN'S MEDAL

Awarded for destroying three enemy vehicles with a medium tank. The targets must be at least two tiers higher than the player's tank.

Alexander Oskin, a Hero of the Soviet Union, was a tank commander who destroyed three King Tigers with his T-34 during a reconnaissance operation near Oglenduv on 11 August, 1944.

PASCUCCI'S MEDAL

Awarded for the destruction of three enemy self-propelled guns.

Second Lieutenant Luigi Arbib Pascucci was an Italian tank commander during World War II. He fought with the Ariete Tank Division in North Africa. Pascucci fought in the Second Battle of El Alamein, where he sacrificed his life in a reckless frontal attack that enabled the rest of his company to escape encirclement.

KOLOBANOV'S MEDAL

Awarded to a player who stands alone against five or more enemy tanks or self-propelled guns and wins (this means that you can capture the enemy base by yourself when you are against five enemies and you will recieve the achievement.)

Colonel Zinoviy Kolobanov was a Soviet tank ace who destroyed 22 German tanks, two guns and two halftracks with his KV in battle on 19 August, 1941.

RADLEY-WALTERS' MEDAL

Awarded to players in Tiers 5 or higher for destroying eight or nine enemy vehicles in one battle.

Sydney Valpy Radley-Walters was a Canadian tank ace of the 27th Armoured Regiment. In 1944–1945 he destroyed 18 German vehicles with his Sherman Firefly.

DUMITRU'S MEDAL

Awarded for the destruction of four enemy self-propelled guns.

Ion S. Dumitru was a Romanian tank ace. He fought in World War II for just twenty-five days, of which five on the German side, and, after Romania changed sides, twenty days against the Germans. On 6 March, 1945, Dumitru contributed to the destruction of six enemy tank destroyers and capture of a battery of 150 mm guns.

BRUNO'S MEDAL

Awarded to players who destroy three or four enemy vehicles and survive the battle to victory despite receiving at least five different critical hits and 80% or more loss of hit points.

Pietro Bruno was an Italian tank ace. For exceptional valor in the face of the enemy he was awarded the Gold Medal of Military Valour (Medaglia d'oro al Valore Militare), the highest Italian award.

BURDA'S MEDAL

Awarded for the destruction of five or more enemy self-propelled guns.

Guards Colonel Alexander Burda was a Soviet tank ace and a Hero of the Soviet Union. On 4 October, 1941, Burda organized an ambush and destroyed an enemy armored column, including 10 medium and light tanks, two trucks with antitank guns and five infantry vehicles. Not awarded to SPG drivers.

NAIDIN'S MEDAL

Awarded to a player who has destroyed all enemy light tanks in a battle (where the enemy team had at least three light tanks). Can be obtained in Random Battles only.

Grigory Nikolaevich Naidin was a sergeant who commanded a BT-7 tank and was a hero of Soviet Union. On 25 July 1941 near Rudyashki village (Lithuania), he destroyed a column of enemy armoured vehicles that consisted of 15 tanks and 10 guns of the 19th Wehrmacht Tank Brigade. This stopped German forces for two days, allowing the Soviets to prepare proper defences for Vilno city.

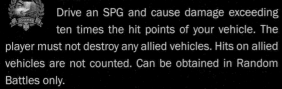

GORE'S MEDAL

Drive an SPG and cause damage exceeding ten times the hit points of your vehicle. The player must not destroy any allied vehicles. Hits on allied vehicles are not counted. Can be obtained in Random Battles only.

British colonel Adrian Clements Gore was in charge of a combat team that defended the Kasserine Pass, Tunisia, on 20 February 1943. His force, composed of a tank squadron, an infantry company and a battery of infantry support artillery, put up stiff resistance against troops of the Wehrmacht Africa Korps, comprising five infantry batallions and one tank batallion. The German forces lost 11 tanks in the fighting.

STARK'S MEDAL

While driving an SPG, destroy at least two enemy vehicles and receive at least two enemy hits that cause damage or are blocked by armor. Survive a battle. Total amount of damage received and damage blocked by armour must be at least 2/3 of the hit points of your vehicle. Hits on allied vehicles are not counted. Can be obtained in Random Battles only.

Colonel Alexander Stark commanded the joint French-American task force defending the Kasserine Pass, Tunisia. On 19 February 1943, Stark's force unleashed heavy artillery fire from the heights surrounding the pass and was able to delay the advancing tank batallion and two infantry batallions of the Wehrmacht Africa Korps, forcing them to request reinforcements.

SPECIAL ACHIEVEMENTS

MASTER GUNNER

Achieve at least five armour penetrating hits in a row against enemy vehicles. The results of the next battle in a row using any vehicle also count towards this number, unless the sequence is broken by a miss, non-penetration or ricochet. The icon in the Service Record displays the longest sequence.

HUNTER

Destroy 100 or more of the following tanks: Aufklärungspanzer Panther, PzKpfw V Panther, Panther II, Panther/M10, Jagdpanther, Jagdpanther II, G.W. Panther, PzKpfw VI Tiger, PzKpfw VI Tiger (P), PzKpfw Tiger II, Jagdtiger, 8.8 cm PaK 43 Jagdtiger, G.W. Tiger, G.W. Tiger (P), Löwe, Leopard prototype A and Leopard 1.

THE LION OF SINAI

Destroy at least 100 tanks of the IS series, and vehicles based on their chassis: IS, IS-3, IS-4, IS-6, IS-7, IS-8, ISU-152, Object 704, Object 261, Object 268 or Object 263.

PATTON VALLEY

Destroy 100 Patton tanks, including M46 Patton, M48A1 Patton III, or M60.

REAPER

Destroy three or more enemy vehicles in a row with a single round each. The achievement is granted on completion of the sequence. The sequence can be continued in the next battle fought on any vehicle. The icon in the Service Record displays the longest sequence.

KAMIKAZE

Destroy a higher-tier enemy vehicle by ramming it. You can only earn this achievement once per battle. The icon in the Service Record displays the number of times the achievement was awarded.

MOUSE TRAP
Destroy ten or more PzKpfw VIII Maus tanks. The icon in the Service Record displays the number of times the achievement was awarded.

BOMBARDIER
Awarded to the player who destroys two or more vehicles with one shot. Can be earned multiple times in one battle.

SHARPSHOOTER
Hit an enemy vehicle ten or more times in a row without missing. The results of the next battle in a row using any vehicle also count towards this number, unless the sequence is broken by a miss. The Service Record icon displays the longest sequence.

INVINCIBLE
Survive five or more consecutive battles without taking any damage (not including battles fought using self-propelled guns). Battles fought using self-propelled guns do not break the sequence, but are not included either. The icon in the Service Record displays the longest sequence.

SURVIVOR
Survive 20 or more consecutive battles. Battles fought using self-propelled guns do not break the sequence, but are not included either.

RAIDER
Capture the enemy base and remain undetected during the entire battle. The icon in the Service Record displays the number of times the achievement was awarded.

FOR COUNTER-BATTERY FIRE
In a battle, destroy all enemy SPGs (at least three) with an SPG. The player must not destroy any allied vehicles. Can be obtained in Random Battles only.

COLD-BLOODED
Destroy at least two enemy light tanks from a distance of not more than 100 metres. Drive a SPG of at least Tier IV. The player must not destroy any allied vehicles. Can be obtained in Random Battles only.

MASTER TANKER
Destroy at least one of every type of enemy vehicle currently available in the game. The icon appears grey in the player's Service Record until the achievement is awarded. Once received, it remains "coloured" even when new tanks are added to the tech trees in game.

EXPERT: U.S.A.
Destroy at least one of each type from the American tech tree. The icon appears grey in the player's Service Record until the achievement is awarded. Once received, it remains "coloured" even when new tanks are added to the tech trees in game.

EXPERT: GERMANY
Destroy at least one of each type from the German tech tree. The icon appears grey in the player's Service Record until the achievement is awarded. Once received, it remains "coloured" even when new tanks are added to the tech trees in game.

EXPERT: FRANCE
Destroy at least one of each type from the French tech tree. The icon appears grey in the player's Service Record until the achievement is awarded. Once received, it remains "coloured" even when new tanks are added to the tech trees in game.

EXPERT: U.S.S.R.
Destroy at least one of each type from the Soviet tech tree. The icon appears grey in the player's Service Record until the achievement is awarded. Once received, it remains "coloured" even when new tanks are added to the tech trees in game.

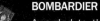

EXPERT: UNITED KINGDOM

Destroy at least one of each type from the United Kingdom tech tree. The icon appears grey in the player's Service Record until the achievement is awarded. Once received, it remains "coloured" even when new tanks are added to the tech trees in game.

EXPERT: CHINA

Destroy at least one of each type from the Chinese tech tree. The icon appears grey in the player's Service Record until the achievement is awarded. Once received, it remains "coloured" even when new tanks are added to the tech trees in game.

SENIOR TECHNICAL ENGINEER

Research all vehicles in all tech trees. In the event that new vehicles are added to any tech tree, the icon becomes grey in the player's Service Record.

TECHNICAL ENGINEER, U.S.A.

Research all vehicles in the American tech tree. In the event that new vehicles are added, the icon becomes grey in the player's Service Record.

TECHNICAL ENGINEER, GERMANY

Research all vehicles in the German tech tree. In the event that new vehicles are added to the tech tree, the icon becomes grey in the player's Service Record.

TECHNICAL ENGINEER, FRANCE

Research all vehicles in the French tech tree. In the event that new vehicles are added to the tech tree, the icon becomes grey in the player's Service Record.

TECHNICAL ENGINEER, U.S.S.R.

Research all vehicles in the Soviet tech tree. In the event that new vehicles are added to the tech tree, the icon becomes grey in the player's Service Record.

TECHNICAL ENGINEER, UNITED KINGDOM

Research all vehicles in the United Kingdom tech tree. In the event that new vehicles are added to the tech tree, the icon becomes grey in the player's Service Record.

TECHNICAL ENGINEER, CHINA

Research all vehicles in the Chinese tech tree. In the event that new vehicles are added to the tech tree, the icon becomes grey in the player's Service Record.

STEP ACHIEVEMENTS

KAY'S MEDAL

Awarded for achieving the Battle Hero status in four classes:

CLASS IV	CLASS III	CLASS II	CLASS I
One time	10 times	100 times	1,000 times

Douglas Kay, a British Army sergeant, and gunner on a Sherman Firefly, participated in the Allied landing in Normandy and was famous for the popularization of the history of tank warfare.

Note: Only the medals listed under "Battle Hero Achievements" above are counted in the "Kay's Medal" achievement.

KNISPEL'S MEDAL

Awarded for the total amount of damage caused and received in four classes:

CLASS IV	CLASS III	CLASS II	HP CLASS I
10,000 HP	100,000 HP	1,000,000	10,000,000 HP

Kurt Knispel, a German tank ace during World War II, participated in battles on both the Western and Eastern Fronts fighting on PzKpfw II, Pzkpfw III, PzKpfw IV, PzKpfw VI Tiger, and PzKpfw Tiger II.

CARIUS' MEDAL

Awarded for the destruction of enemy tanks and self-propelled guns in four classes:

CLASS IV	CLASS III	CLASS II	CLASS I
10 vehicles	100 vehicles	1,000 vehicles	10,000 vehicles

Otto Carius was one of the most efficient tank aces of World War II. He commanded the PzKpfw 38 (t), the PzKpfw VI Tiger and the Jagdtiger tank destroyer during his impressive career.

POPEL'S MEDAL

Awarded for detecting enemy tanks and self-propelled guns in all battles, in four classes:

CLASS IV	CLASS III	CLASS II	CLASS I
20 vehicles	200 vehicles	2,000 vehicles	20,000 vEHICLES

Lieutenant General of Tank Forces, Nikolai Popel, a Soviet military leader and political worker, organized a raid against the enemy rear using captured vehicles during the battle of Dubno in the Summer of 1941.

ABRAMS' MEDAL

Awarded in one of four classes for the total number of team victories in which the player survived the battle:

CLASS IV	CLASS III	CLASS II	CLASS I
Five victories	50 victories	500 victories	5,000 victories

General Creighton Abrams commanded U.S. armoured forces during World War II and the Vietnam War, earning a reputation as an aggressive and successful commander.

LECLERC'S MEDAL

Awarded for the total amount of the player's enemy base capture points. An unsuccessful or reduced capture does not count toward this number. The award is established in four classes:

CLASS IV	CLASS III	CLASS II	CLASS I
Three vehicles	30 vehicles	300 vehicles	3,000 vehicles

Philippe Leclerc was a General of the Free French Forces during World War II and one of the leaders of the Paris liberation operation

LAVRINENKO'S MEDAL

Awarded for reducing the total number of capture points of a friendly base, up to 100 points per battle. This award is established in four classes:

CLASS IV	CLASS III	CLASS II	CLASS I
30 points	300 points	3,000 points	30,000 points

Dmitry Lavrinenko, a Hero of the Soviet Union, Guards Lieutenant, and tank ace was recognized as the most efficient Soviet tanker, destroying 52 tanks in 28 battles over the course of just two months.

EKINS' MEDAL

Awarded in four classes for destroying Tier VIII, IX or X enemy tanks and self-propelled guns:

CLASS IV	CLASS III	CLASS II	CLASS I
3 vehicles	30 vehicles	300 vehicles	3,000 vehicles

Joe Ekins was a private in the Northamptonshire Division of the British Territorial Army. A number of sources confirm Ekins as the final nemesis of famous German tank ace Michael Wittmann.

CLAN WARS: RISE OF THE AMERICAS ACHIEVEMENTS

FEELIN' PEACHY
Awarded to each member of the clan which, after the first day of the Rise of the Americas: Unclaimed Glory event, had captured the province of Atlanta, Georgia.

DEEP DISH DELIVERY
Awarded to each member of the clan which, after the first day of the Rise of the Americas: Unclaimed Glory event, had captured the province of Chicago, Illinois.

NO SLEEP TILL BROOKLYN
Awarded to each member of the clan which won the No Sleep Till Brooklyn Rumble.

Note: this award was originally intended for each member of the clan which, after the first day of the Rise of the Americas: Unclaimed Glory event, had captured the province of New York City, New York. However, in the end, the final battle ended in a draw and New York City lay unclaimed. The No Sleep Till Brooklyn Rumble tournament was held February 1–3, 2013, and the medal was awarded to the victors.

SHOW ME THE MONEY
Awarded to each member of the clan which, after the first day of the Rise of the Americas: Unclaimed Glory event, had captured the province of Riverlands, Missouri.

HOME OF THE BRAVES
Awarded to each member of the clan which, after the end of Rise of the Americas Stage 1, held the province of Atlanta, Georgia.

CAPWNED
Awarded to each member of the clan which, after the end of Americas Stage 1, held the province of Chicago, Illinois.

FUHGEDDABOUDIT
Awarded to each member of the clan which, after the end of Rise of the Americas Stage 1, held the province of New York City, New York.

THE MIGHTY MO
Awarded to each member of the clan which, after the end of Rise of the Americas Stage 1, held the province of Riverlands, Missouri.

MESSED WITH TEXAS
Awarded to each member of the clan which, after the end of Rise of the Americas Stage II, held the province of San Antonio, Texas.

RUSHMORE, CAPFAST
Awarded to each member of the clan which, after the end of Rise of the Americas Stage II, held the province of Missouri Plateau, South Dakota.

BUTTING HEADS
Awarded to each member of the clan which, after the end of Rise of the Americas Stage II, held the province of Big Horn, Wyoming.

MILE HIGH RANGER
Awarded to each member of the clan which, after the end of Rise of the Americas Stage II, held the province of Front Range, Colorado.

NEEDS MORE SALT
Awarded to each member of the clan which, after the end of Rise of the Americas Stage III, held the province of Ogden, Utah.

TANKZ N THE HOOD
Awarded to each member of the clan which, after the end of Rise of the Americas Stage III, held the province of Hood, Oregon.

SAND CRAWLERS
Awarded to each member of the clan which, after the end of Rise of the Americas Stage III, held the province of Death Valley, California.

BRAVE NEW WORLD
Awarded to each member of the clan which, held any land in the U.S. at any time during the whole event of Rise of the Americas.

CLAN WARS: FIRST CAMPAIGN ACHIEVEMENTS

LEGENDARY
Awarded to each member of the top clan of a Clan Wars Campaign.

CAMPAIGN PARTICIPANT
Awarded to players who participated in at least one battle during a Clan Wars Campaign.

INDESTRUCTIBLE
Awarded to each member of the second place clan of a Clan Wars Campaign.

NEVERMORE MEDAL
Awarded to the members of the clan who owned the Maryland Province at the end of Clan Wars Campaign Stage: Landlords.

VETERAN
Awarded to each member of the third place clan of a Clan Wars Campaign.

GATEKEEPERS MEDAL
Awarded to the members of the clan who owned the Prince Albert Island Province at the end of Clan Wars Campaign Stage: Landlords.

BY IRON AND BLOOD
Awarded to members of the clan with the highest total Victory Points by the end of Clan Wars Campaigns Stage One: Landlords.

WHITE FANG MEDAL
Awarded to the members of the clan who owned the Klondike Province at the end of Clan Wars Campaign Stage: Landlords.

MAGNATE
Awarded to members of the clan with the highest total Victory Points by the end of Clan Wars Campaigns Stage Two: Rise and Fall.

EXPULSION AND PLUNDER MEDAL
Awarded to members of the clan receiving the largest amount of Gold ransacking provinces during Clan Wars Campaigns Stage Two: Rise and Fall.

IRON FIST
Awarded to members of the clan with the highest total Victory Points by the end of Clan Wars Campaigns Stage III: Revolution Epoch.

CRUSHER MEDAL
Awarded to members of the clan who removes (by conquering their last province) the most clans from the Global Map during Clan Wars Campaigns Stage IV: World Domination.

ULTIMATE SUPREMACY
Awarded to members of the clan receiving the largest amount of VP during Clan Wars Campaigns Stage IV: World Domination.

WITH FIRE AND SWORD MEDAL
Awarded to members of the clan who pacifies the largest number of riots during Clan Wars Campaigns Stage III: Revolution Epoch.

CLAN WARS:
SECOND CAMPAIGN ACHIEVEMENTS

TRIUMPHATOR I CLASS MEDAL
Awarded to the members of the clan that takes first place in Clan Wars: Second Campaign, based on the amount of Victory Points.

TRIUMPHATOR II CLASS MEDAL
Awarded to the members of the clan that takes second place in Clan Wars: Second Campaign, based on the amount of Victory Points.

TRIUMPHATOR III CLASS MEDAL
Awarded to the members of the clan that takes third place in Clan Wars: Second Campaign, based on the amount of Victory Points.

EMPEROR MEDAL
Awarded to the members of the clan who won the First Stage: Revolution Epoch (Tier I-VI)) of Clan Wars: Second Campaign.

NOMAD MEDAL
Awarded to the members of the clan who won the Second Stage: Train Robbery (Tier I-VIII) of Clan Wars: Second Campaign.

GOLD DIGGER MEDAL
Awarded to the members of the clan who won the Third Stage: Gold Rush (Tier I-X) of Clan Wars: Second Campaign.

2ND CAMPAIGN COMPETITOR'S RIBBON
Awarded to all players who participated in at least one battle in each Stage of Clan Wars: Second Campaign.

VEHICLES

LIGHT

T1 CUNNINGHAM (I)

M2 LIGHT TANK (II)

T1E6 (II)

T2 LIGHT TANK (II)

T7 COMBAT CAR (II)

M22 LOCUST (III)

M3 STUART(III)

MTLS-1G14 (III)

M5 STUART (IV)

M24 CHAFFEE (V)

T21 (VI)

T37 (VI)

M41 WALKER BULLDOG (VII)

T71 (VII)

T49 (VIII)

BRITISH

CRUISER MK. I (II)

M2 (II)

CRUISER MK. III (II)

LIGHT MK. VIC (II)

STUART I-IV (III)

CRUISER MK. IV (III)

CRUISER MK. II (III)

VALENTINE (IV)

COVENANTER (IV)

CRUSADER (V)

GERMAN

LEICHTTRAKTOR (I)

PZ.KPFW. II AUSF. D (II)

PZ.KPFW. 38H 735 (F) (II)

PZ.KPFW. 35 (T) (II)

PZ.KPFW. I (II)

PZ.KPFW. II (II)

PZ.KPFW. 38 (T) (III)

PZ.KPFW. III AUSF. A (III)

PZ.KPFW. II AUSF. J (III)

PZ.KPFW. I AUSF. C (III)

PZ.KPFW. II AUSF. G (III)

T-15 (III)

PZ.KPFW. 38 (T) N.A. (IV)

PZ.KPFW. II LUCHS (IV)

VK 16.02 LEOPARD (V)

VK 28.01 (VI)

AUFKLÄRUNGSPANZER
PANTHER (VII)

SPÄHPANZER RU 251 (VIII)

RENAULT FT (I)

D1 (II)

FCM 36 (II)

RENAULT R35 (II)

HOTCHKISS H35 (II)

AMX 38 (III)

AMX 40 (IV)

AMX ELC BIS (V)

AMX 12 T (VI)

AMX 13 75 (VII)

AMX 13 57 GF (VII)

AMX 13 90 (VIII)

SOVIET

MS-1 (I)

BT-2 (II)

T-26 (II)

T-60 (II)

TETRARCH (II)

BT-7 (III)

BT-SV (III)

LTP (III)

M3 LIGHT (III)

T-127 (III)

T-46 (III)

T-70 (III)

A-20 (IV)

T-50 (IV)

T-80 (IV)

VALENTINE II (IV)

MT-25 (VI)

LTTB (VII)

T-54 LTWT. (VIII)

CHINESE

RENAULT NC-31 (I)

VICKERS MK. E TYPE B (II)

TYPE 2597 CHI-HA (III)

M5A1 STUART (IV)

59-16 (VI)

TYPE 64 (VI)

TYPE 62 (VII)

WZ-131 (VII)

WZ-132 (VIII)

JAPANESE

RENAULT OTSU (I)

TYPE 95 HA-GO (II)

TYPE 97 TE-KE (II)

TYPE 98 KE-NI (III)

TYPE 5 KE-HO (IV)

MEDIUM

 ## AMERICAN

T2 MEDIUM TANK (II)

M2 MEDIUM
TANK (III)

M3 LEE (IV)

M4A2E4 SHERMAN (V)

M4 SHERMAN (V)

M7 (V)

RAM II (V)

M4A3E8 FURY (VI)

M4A3E8 SHERMAN (VI)

M4A3E2 SHERMAN
JUMBO (VI)

T20 (VII)

T23E3 (VII)

M26 PERSHING (VIII)

T26E4
SUPERPERSHING (VIII)

T69 (VIII)

T95E2 (VIII)

INDIEN-PAN...

M46 PATTON (IX)

T54E1 (IX)

M48A1 PATTON (X)

M60 (X)

LEOPARD PROTO...

BRITISH

FR...

VICKERS MEDIUM MK. I (I)

VICKERS MEDIUM MK. II (II)

VICKERS MEDIUM MK. III (III)

MATILDA (IV)

D2 (III)

GRANT (IV)

SHERMAN III (V)

MATILDA BLACK PRINCE (V)

SHERMAN FIREFLY (VI)

AMX CHASSEUR DE C...

CROMWELL (VI)

CROMWELL B (VI)

COMET (VII)

CENTURION MK. I (VIII)

AMX 30 B (X)

CENTURION MK. 7/1 (IX)

FV4202 (X)

SOVIET

A-32 (IV)

GROSSTR

PZ.KPFW. I

PZ.KPFW. IV

PZ.KPFW. V/IV

PANTHER/M

T-28 (IV)

MATILDA IV (V)

T-34 (V)

A-43 (VI)

T-34-85M (VI)

T-34-85 RUDY (VI)

T-34-85 (VI)

A-44 (VII)

KV-13 (VII)

T-43 (VII)

T-44-122 (VII)

OBJECT 416 (VIII)

T-54 FIRST PROTOTYPE (VIII)

T-44 (VIII)

OBJECT 430 VERSION II (IX)

T-54 (IX)

OBJECT 140 (X)

OBJECT 430 (X)

OBJECT 907 (X)

T-62A (X)

CHINESE

TYPE T-34 (V)

TYPE 58 (VI)

T-34-1 (VII)

TYPE 59 (VIII)

T-34-2 (VIII)

T-34-3 (VIII)

WZ-120 (IX)

121 (X)

JAPANESE

CHI-NI (II)

TYPE 97 CHI-HA (III)

TYPE 1 CHI-HE (IV)

TYPE 3 CHI-NU (V)

TYPE 3 CHI-NU KAI (V)

TYPE 4 CHI-TO (VI)

TYPE 5 CHI-RI (VII)

STA-1 (VIII)

STA-2 (VIII)

TYPE 61 (IX)

STB-1 (X)

HEAVY

T14 (V) T1 HEAVY TANK (V) M6 (VI) T29 (VII)

M6A2E1 (VIII) T32 (VIII) T34 (VIII) M103 (IX)

T110E5 (X) T57 HEAVY TANK (X)

BRITISH

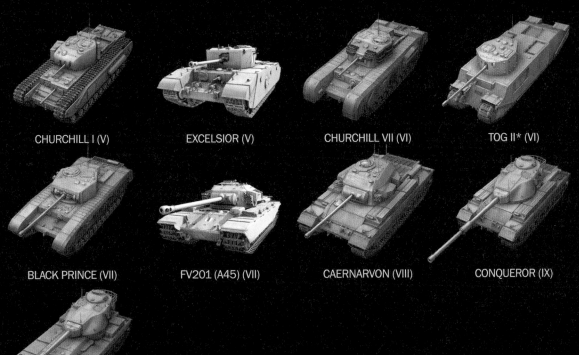

CHURCHILL I (V)

EXCELSIOR (V)

CHURCHILL VII (VI)

TOG II* (VI)

BLACK PRINCE (VII)

FV201 (A45) (VII)

CAERNARVON (VIII)

CONQUEROR (IX)

FV215B (X)

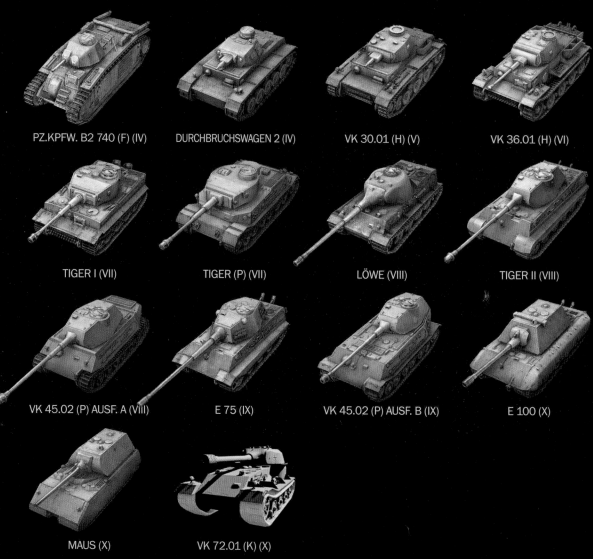

PZ.KPFW. B2 740 (F) (IV)   DURCHBRUCHSWAGEN 2 (IV)   VK 30.01 (H) (V)   VK 36.01 (H) (VI)

TIGER I (VII)   TIGER (P) (VII)   LÖWE (VIII)   TIGER II (VIII)

VK 45.02 (P) AUSF. A (VIII)   E 75 (IX)   VK 45.02 (P) AUSF. B (IX)   E 100 (X)

MAUS (X)   VK 72.01 (K) (X)

B1 (IV)   BDR G1 B (V)   ARL 44 (VI)   AMX M4 MLE. 45 (VII)

AMX 50 100 (VIII)   FCM 50 T (VIII)   AMX 50 120 (IX)   AMX 50 B (X)

SOVIET

CHURCHILL III (V)   KV-1S (V)   KV-220 (V)   KV-220 BETA-TEST (V)

KV-1 (V)   KV-2 (VI)   KV-85 (VI)   T-150 (VI)

IS (VII)

KV-3 (VII)

IS-2 (VII)

IS-3 (VIII)

IS-6 (VIII)

KV-5

KV-4 (VIII)

IS-5 (OBJECT 730) (VIII)

IS-8 (IX)

ST-I (IX)

IS-4 (X)

IS-7 (X)

OBJECT 260 (X)

CHINESE

IS-2 (VII)

WZ-111 (VIII)

110 (VIII)

112 (VIII)

WZ-111 MODEL 1-4 (IX)

113 (IX)

TANK DESTROYERS

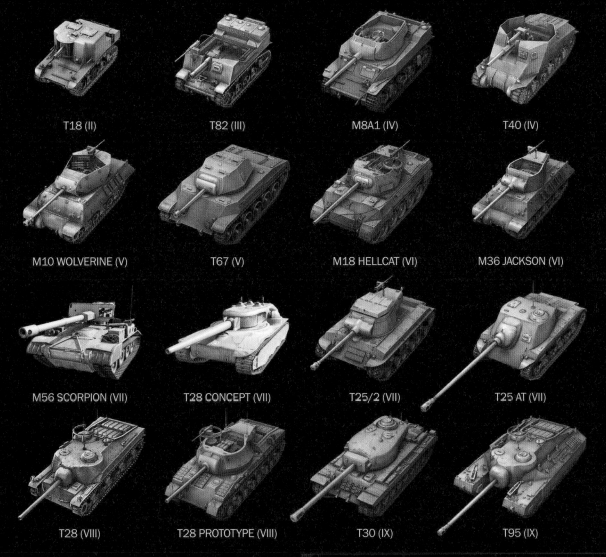

T18 (II)

T82 (III)

M8A1 (IV)

T40 (IV)

M10 WOLVERINE (V)

T67 (V)

M18 HELLCAT (VI)

M36 JACKSON (VI)

M56 SCORPION (VII)

T28 CONCEPT (VII)

T25/2 (VII)

T25 AT (VII)

T28 (VIII)

T28 PROTOTYPE (VIII)

T30 (IX)

T95 (IX)

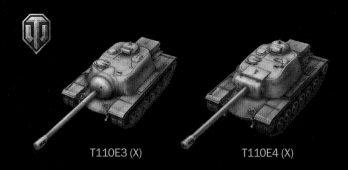

T110E3 (X)

T110E4 (X)

BRITISH

UNIVERSAL CARRIER
2-PDR (II)

VALENTINE AT (III)

ALECTO (IV)

ARCHER (V)

AT 2 (V)

CHURCHILL GUN CARRIER (VI)

ACHILLES (VI)

AT 8 (VI)

CHALLENGER (VII)

AT 15A (VII)

AT 7 (VII)

AT 15 (VIII)

CHARIOTEER (VIII)

TORTOISE (IX)

FV4004 CONWAY (IX)

FV215B (183) (X)

FV4005 STAGE II (X)

GERMAN

PANZERJÄGER I (II)

MARDER II (III)

STUG III AUSF. B (IV)

HETZER (IV)

MARDER 38T (IV)

STUG IV (V)

PZ.SFL. IVC (V)

STUG III AUSF. G (V)

DICKER MAX (VI)

JAGDPANZER IV (VI)

NASHORN (VI)

E 25 (VII)

JAGDPANTHER (VII)

STURER EMIL (VII)

FERDINAND (VIII)

JAGDPANTHER II (VIII)

JAGDTIGER (IX)

JAGDPANZER E 100 (X)

WAFFENTRÄGER AUF E 100 (X)

8,8 CM PAK 43 JAGDTIGER (VIII)

RHM.-BORSIG
WAFFENTRÄGER (VIII)

WAFFENTRÄGER AUF PZ.
IV (IX)

FRENCH

RENAULT FT AC (II)

FCM 36 PAK 40 (III)

RENAULT UE 57 (III)

SOMUA SAU 40 (IV)

S35 CA (V)

ARL V39 (VI)

AMX AC MLE. 46 (VII)

AMX AC MLE. 48 (VIII)

SOVIET

AT-1 (II)

SU-76 (III)

SU-76I (III)

SU-85B (IV)

SU-85 (V)

SU-85I (V)

SU-100 (VI)

SU-100Y (VI)

ISU-122S (VII)

SU-152 (VII)

SU-100M1 (VII)

SU-122-44 (VII)

ISU-152 (VIII)

ISU-130 (VIII)

SU-101 (VIII)

OBJECT 704 (IX)

SU-122-54 (IX)

OBJECT 263 (X)

OBJECT 268 (X)

SPGs

T57 (II)

M7 PRIEST (III)

M37 (IV)

M41 HMC (V)

M44 (VI)

M12 (VII)

M40/M43 (VIII)

M53/M55 (IX)

T92 (X)

BRITISH

LOYD GUN CARRIAGE (II)

SEXTON II (III)

SEXTON I (III)

BIRCH GUN (IV)

BISHOP (V)

FV304 (VI)

CRUSADER 5.5-IN. SP (VII)

FV207 (VIII)

FV3805 (IX)

CONQUEROR GUN
CARRIAGE (X)

GERMAN

G.PZ. MK. VI (E) (II)

STURMPANZER I BISON (III)

WESPE (III)

PZ.SFL. IVB (IV)

STURMPANZER II (IV)

GRILLE (V)

HUMMEL (VI)

G.W. PANTHER (VII)

G.W. TIGER (P) (VIII)

G.W. TIGER (IX)

G.W. E 100 (X)

 FRENCH

RENAULT FT 75 BS (II)

LORRAINE 39L AM (III)

AMX 105 AM MLE. 47 (IV)

AMX 13 105 AM MLE. 50 (V)

105 LEFH18B2 (V)

AMX 13 F3 AM (VI)

LORRAINE 155 MLE.
50 (VII)

LORRAINE 155 MLE.
51 (VIII)

BAT.-CHÂTILLON 155
55 (IX)

BAT.-CHÂTILLON 155
58 (X)

SOVIET

SU-18 (II)

SU-26 (III)

SU-5 (IV)

SU-122A (V)

SU-8 (VI)

S-51 (VII)

SU-14-1 (VII)

SU-14-2 (VIII)

212A (IX)

OBJECT 261 (X)

LET THE ULTIMAT
CONQUES
BEGIN

CLAN WARS

Clan Wars is World of Tanks' high level metagame, a way of stringing together a series of battles into a wider context. Players form into large clans and play out games on a turn-based map, moving to capture territories. When a clan encroaches on another clan's territory a battle time is set.

Clan Wars actions are taken by the clan commander or their officers on the Global Map. Here they can elect to attack a "front", which is a collection of "provinces" to be fought over. So, if your clan elects to assault a front, then they can't be attacked by clans from adjacent fronts. You simultaneously attack many fronts if you think your clan is big enough to handle it! Different fronts have different restrictions on how many players can fight on a team and what the maximum tier of tanks allowed is, so you may want to attack both a high and low level front so that all members of your clan can get involved.

There are two ways to land in a front if you aren't already fighting there, the first is via an auction, the second is by winning a tournament. Auctions involve the different factions who want to land there bidding influence against each other. Clans have no idea what the other bids are or even if there are any. The province owner can also make 'defensive bids' to try and avoid an attack by the auction winner. Win the auction and your division lands in the province, contesting it as you would if you'd attacked from an adjacent territory. Alternatively, provinces might be flagged for tournament entry, any team that doesn't already have a presence in that front can enter, and they all go into a tournament to decide who goes forward.

At this point, these landing clans are then put into a tournament with all the clans who attacked a province by land (see below). The winner goes on to face the province owner for control of the territory. Battles take place at 'prime time', and each front has several groups of provinces that share the same time. At one hour before prime time

all map actions in the province are suspended, and only become unlocked again once the battles have ended. It is the clan's duty to have enough people online to actually fight their battles when prime time comes around.

In order to assault an adjacent territory by land, you need to move a division into it. Divisions are the basic attacking unit of Clan Wars. You get one for free when you land on a front, but if you want any more you have to buy them with influence. Modules can also be purchased to give your divisions extra boosts, like increased sight ranges. Adding modules to your division increases its upkeep cost. To attack a territory you need to either move a division into it or land on it. To defend a territory you must have a division in it. If you don't have a division in your territory come prime time, you will automatically lose it to the winner of the attacker's tournament!

Holding a province earns your clan gold. This goes into the clan treasury and can be used to pay for clan actions. The other major resource in Clan Wars is influence. Influence is earned by taking part in stronghold skirmishes and global map battles, and can be used to organze and maintain divisions and modules.

Clan Wars is a huge and complex part of high level World of Tanks play, akin to joining a raiding guild in an MMO. I've only scratched the surface here, because you're not likely to get involved until at least Tier VI, but if you feel ready for it your best bet is to join an existing clan and let your clanmates teach you the ropes. Good luck!

Command Center

Level III

| Durability | 1 500 / 1 500 |
| Storage | 279 / 2 340 |

Zones of Stronghold

Open Zones allow the building of structures, where Reserves are requested. Zones can be attacked by enemy clans.

Zones open: 2 — Zone Control

Garrison: 23

STRONGHOLDS

Strongholds are a relatively new part of Clan Wars designed to give clans a slightly more accessible, pick up and play alternative to global map battles. Only a clan commander can build a stronghold, but once they do, the executive officer can manage it as well, building various structures inside to improve the clan's rewards. There are three kinds of stronghold battle: attack, defend or skirmish. Skirmish offers consequence free resources that anyone can participate in. You can also attack other clan's stronghold, but making yourself eligible to attack also means you'll have to defend your stronghold against other attacks. These battles can be fought at several scales, be it between seven Tier VI tanks or 15 Tier X tanks.

Winning stronghold battles gets you industrial reserve, which can be fed into stronghold buildings to create boosters for your clan called 'reserves'. For example, the Tankodrome creates 'tactical training' which boosts the experience earned by all clan members after a battle. There are also airstrikes and artillery strikes that offer an in battle edge, but can only be used during stronghold attacks.

STARTING YOUR OWN CLAN

As well as joining an existing clan, you can start one yourself. Forming a clan costs 2,500, and it only takes one person to do so, who automatically becomes the clan commander. At this point you can invite as many friends as you like to join your clan, up to 100, but you'll need at least 15 to show up in the clan ratings and fight battles. You'll get to name you clan, add a motto, logo and a 2–5 character tag that appears after the names of all members. You'll also be able to allocate the gold earned by the clan, perform actions on the global map, appoint officers and much more. Officers are other clan members who can also perform some of these actions. For example, the executive officer can do everything a clan commander can do except disband the clan, while a recruitment officer deals specifically with adding new members and the quartermaster allocates the clan's hard earned gold.

TOURNAMENTS

World of Tanks e-sports tournaments happen regularly, once a week at least, and offer players the chance to participate in competitive, highly organized matches with tight restrictions for big prizes. Usually the prize is gold, ranging anywhere from 100 to 20,000, but occasionally even for cash.

Tournaments play very differently to Random Battles in several ways, namely:

- ▶ The teams are organized, not random (obviously).
- ▶ Matches are shorter, generally lasting seven or 10 minutes instead of 15.
- ▶ There will be tight restrictions on what tanks can be used. Usually this takes the form of tier or class restrictions, but sometimes specific tanks will be banned outright.
- ▶ Tournaments are played at specific times, they are not 'pick up and play'.
- ▶ All battles for a tournament will usually take place on one map or a small collection of maps rather than randomly cycling through the full list.
- ▶ There are no repair costs for participating in a tournament, but ammunition and consumables must be paid for as normal.
- ▶ There are no credit or experience rewards for tournament games, but winning the tournament usually confers a prize in gold.

When a tournament is announced, anyone can create a team, automatically becoming the team captain. At that point the captain sets about recruiting people for the team, organizing it however they see fit. Once they're happy with their lineup they must register their team for the tournament. At this point they can no longer change their team, so make sure you've chosen people you can trust to show up! Thankfully you can also name several 'reserves'

1 7000€

1ST PLACE   EVIL PANDA SQUAD "EPS"

2ND PLACE   ODEM MORTIS "OM"

3 2000€

3RD PLACE   1ST PAD EXPENDABLES

WORLD of TANKS
ROLL OUT

(intel) EXTREME MASTERS

KATOWICE / SPODEK
18-20.01.2013

WARGAMING.NET
LET'S BATTLE

to swap in and out if needed in case disaster strikes.

The vast majority of tournaments follow a traditional group stage and playoff structure. If you've ever watch the FIFA World Cup, it's just like that. If you haven't, here's how it goes. Teams are randomly sorted into groups who each play each other once, earning three points for a win, one point for a draw and no points for a loss. The top teams are then put into a knockout tournament to decide the final winner.

There are exceptions of course. The popular "skirmish" tournament type sorts all group stage participants into the top 50% and bottom 50%, with each going into its own sub tournament. The bottom competition obviously has less competition, but also less prizes. Teams can also decide to enter direction into the bottom half competition, skipping the first round entirely.

The key difference between tournaments and regular games is discipline and co-operation. Competitive games are a world apart from public games where everyone is more forgiving of silliness and unorthodox tactics. If you're planning to get involved with e-sports you'll need a solid group of players that you trust and who trust you in return, often found through a clan. It isn't for beginners, but it does make for a rewarding experience.

WARGAMING LEAGUE

The Wargaming league is the official e-sports league for North America and Europe. It is based on a ladder system of several different leagues, with teams promoted and relegated between them. The leagues are set up differently in Europe and North America, so we'll cover them one by one.

IN EUROPE

The Bronze League is the lowest league in Europe, with anyone able to create a team and enter. The top 5 teams are promoted to the Silver League. There is also a Bronze League knockout tournament whose winner gets promoted into Silver.

The Silver League comes next. Unlike the North American Leagues, European Silver League teams receive a stipend for playing based on their position in the league. The top two teams get automatically promoted while the 3rd-6th teams enter compete against relegated Gold League teams for a spot. The lowest six teams drop down into Bronze.

The Gold League is the highest league, with cash prizes and a bigger stipend than the Silver League. The bottom two teams are automatically relegated while other lowest placed teams must play compete against Silver League teams to stay in.

RULES FOR EUROPE

- ► Games are Assault with two capture points
- ► 54 tier points per team
- ► Seven players per team
- ► Maximum ier is VIII
- ► Maps for Europe
- ► Winter Himmelsdorf
- ► Ensk
- ► Ruinsberg
- ► Mines
- ► Steppes
- ► Cliff
- ► Prokhorovka

IN NORTH AMERICA

The Open League is available to anyone who wants to enter by forming a team, alongside those relegated from the Bronze League. There are two divisions within the Open League. The top eight teams are promoted to the Bronze League.

The Bronze League consists of teams that have been promoted from the Open League or relegated from the Silver League. The top five teams are promoted to the Silver League, while the bottom eight drop back down to the Open League. Bronze League battles are first to two wins out of five.

The Silver League is the qualifying league for the prestigious Gold League, consisting of teams promoted from Bronze or relegated from Gold. The top two teams are automatically promoted to the Gold League while the teams ranked 3rd-6th compete against relegated Gold League teams for a spot. The bottom five teams are relegated to the Bronze League. Silver League battles are first to two wins out of five.

The Gold League is the highest league, with two divisions and the promise of cash prizes for the winners. The bottom two teams are automatically relegated while other lowest placed teams must play compete against Silver League teams to stay in. Players also receive a stipend for playing in the Gold League. Gold League battles are best out of five.

RULES FOR NORTH AMERICA

- ► 42 tier points per team
- ► Seven players per team
- ► Maximum Tier is VIII
- ► Maps for North America
- ► Himmelsdorf
- ► Ensk
- ► Ruinsberg
- ► Mines
- ► Steppes
- ► Cliff
- ► Abbey
- ► Prokhorovka

REAL TANKS

This chapter looks at the inspiration behind the vechicles in the game. Most of the tanks on the next few pages are real, although some never progressed beyond the prototype stage.

Valentine

Above: The Valentine was the most produced British tank of World War II with more than 8,000 built, many of which were supplied to the Soviet Union. Developed in conformity with the British "Infantry Tank" concept, it was slow and rugged. However, it was dependable and required relatively little maintenance.

Above right: The T-70 was an effective light tank that was produced in significant numbers by the USSR between January 1942 and October 1943. With more than 8,000 rolling off the production line, it was second in number only to the T-34.

Right: The T-28 entered service with the Soviet Red Army in 1933, and by the time of Operation Barbarossa (June 1941), over 400 were in service. However, it proved difficult to upgrade and was prone to mechanical problems. By the end of 1941, Soviet tank designers had turned their attention to more modern and effective vehicles.

T-70

T-28

T-34-85

Above: In an effort to upgrade the T-34 with more firepower to take on heavier German tanks on the Eastern Front, Soviet designers modified an existing three-man turret and fitted it with an 85mm gun. The new model was a success and almost 39,000 T-34-85s were built from 1944 until the late 1950s.

Above right: The KV-1 entered production in 1939 and at 45 tons was twice as heavy as the largest German tanks it encountered in 1941. Although it was difficult to operate, its thick armour proved almost impervious to vehicle-mounted weapons and gave the Germans a shock during their invasion of Russia.

Right: The IS-8 heavy tank, more heavily armoured than its predecessor the IS-3, entered service in 1953 before being re-designated as the T-10. It remained in production until 1966, but by this time the Red Army had switched to the production of smaller, faster main battle tanks.

KV-1

IS-8

PzKpfw 38H 735 (f)

The German army captured a large number of Hotchkiss H35 tanks in 1940, which they adapted as the Pz.Kpfw. 38H 735 (f). They were mostly deployed for occupation duties in France and other countries.

Leichttraktor

This light tank was developed in secret as the Versailles Treaty prevented Germany from developing new weapons after World War I.

Panther

The Panther featured armour inspired by the Soviet T-34, a Maybach V12 engine and the very effective 7.5cm L/70 gun. It was perhaps the closest that German designers came to realizing the ideal blend of manoeuvrability, protection and firepower, and is regarded as one of the most successful designs of World War II.

PzKpfw II Ausf J

A reconnaissance vehicle with enhanced survivability, this was bigger, heavier and slower than other Panzer II models, earning it the nickname "Little Tiger".

PzKpfw B2 740 (f)

Tiger II

Tiger I

Above: Perhaps the most famous of all German tanks of World War II, the Tiger I was designed with an emphasis on firepower and protection. When it entered service its 88mm gun was the only German weapon that could penetrate T-34 and KV-1 armour at any distance.

Above left: A large number of French heavy B1 tanks were captured by German forces after the fall of France in 1940 and they were put into the service of the German Army. Some were modified for other roles such as self-propelled artillery but most were utilised as armoured vehicles for occupation forces.

Left: The 68-ton Tiger II or *Königstiger* made its combat debut in Normandy in July 1944, and despite being underpowered (it used the same engine as the much lighter Panther and Tiger I), its heavy armour and accurate 8.8cm L/71 gun made it a formidable opponent.

PzKpfw VIII Maus

Above: The largest tank ever built, only two prototypes of the super-heavy Maus were ever produced. The second prototype, completed in early 1944, was armed with both a 128mm and a 75mm gun. The entire tank weighed 288 tonnes; the turret alone weighed the same as a Tiger I.

Above right: The Hetzer was officially known as the Jagdpanzer 38, its design based on a version of the Panzer 38 (t). It was reliable, cost-effective and easy to conceal due to its low profile and relatively small size.

Right: The earliest example of a German tank destroyer, the Panzerjäger I was created by mounting a Skoda 4.7cm gun on to the hull of the obsolete Panzer I Ausf B. The Panzerjäger I performed well against French tanks in 1940 but proved far less effective against the newer and more powerful Russian vehicles it encountered on the Eastern Front.

Hetzer

Panzerjäger I

StuG III

PzSfl IVb

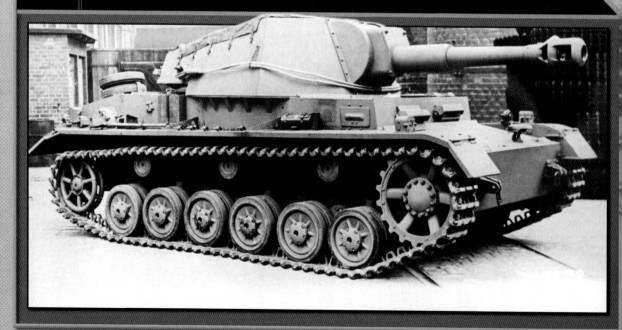

G.W. Panther

Above: The GW Panther was a design concept developed by the German manufacturer Krupp during World War II. Its basis was the Panther hull with a K43 gun mounted at the rear, in an enclosed "turret". A firing platform was designed to be lowered around the rear hull when the gun was brought into action.

Above left: Germany's Stug (*Sturmgeschütz*) line of AFVs was that nation's most produced line of World War II. The Stug III was originally designed as an infantry support vehicle, but as the series developed it was more commonly employed as a tank destroyer.

Left: An 18-ton self-propelled gun designed by Krupp in 1939, the Pz.Sfl. IVb (or Sd.Kfz 165/1) was equipped with a 10.5cm light howitzer and manned by a crew of four. Although the army ordered 200 vehicles, only 8–10 were produced by the end of 1942 and these were sent into service on the Eastern Front.

T49

T2 Medium

M3 Lee

Above: The distinctive M3 Lee was produced in large numbers for both the US and British armies in 1941. It offered firepower but there were drawbacks: the 75mm gun on the hull could not be traversed to the left, it lacked sufficient armour and its high profile made it a large target for German gunners.

Above left: The T49 design was created in 1952 with the aim of combining medium tank firepower with light tank mobility. Designers based it on the M41 Walker Bulldog which they adapted to mount a 90mm gun. The tank never entered service.

Left: An inter-war design fitted with a 47mm gun and weighing only 14 tons, the T2 Medium was largely inspired by the British Vickers Mk II and had a similar type of suspension. It was the basis for the future development of the M2 Light Tank.

Medium Tank T20

Tank Cruiser, Ram Mk II

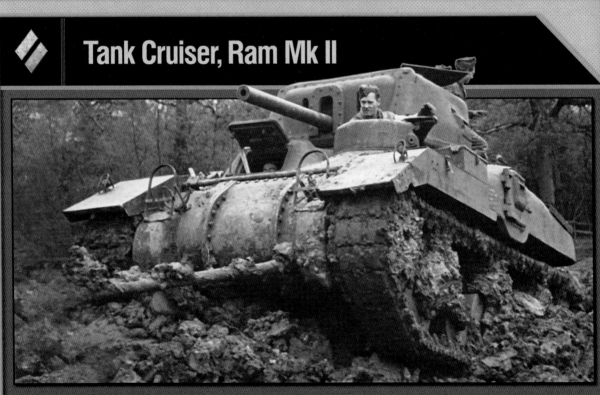

Above: The most widely produced US tank of World War II, the M4 entered service in 1942. It was mobile, reliable and relatively cheap to produce. Although outgunned by heavier German opponents, numerical superiority often handed Sherman crews a crucial advantage.

Above left: Conceived as a successor to the M4 Sherman, a number of different prototypes of the T20 were envisaged. Mechanical problems ensured that none entered production, but development continued, culminating in the M26 Pershing.

Left: The Ram was designed and built in Canada to fill a gap in the armoured component of Canada's armed forces in World War II. The chassis, engine, transmission and suspension were that of the M3 Lee and it carried a British QF 6-pounder gun. i

M60 Patton

The M60 entered service with the US armed forces in 1960 and it remained the Main Battle Tank of the US Army until replaced by the M1 Abrams. The 50-ton design was armed with a 105mm gun and has proven to be adaptable and easily upgraded; hundreds of these tanks remain in service all over the world.

Heavy Tank T29

The T29 was intended as a counter to the German heavy tanks faced by the U.S. Army in Europe. The gun mantlet featured 249mm of armour – in contrast the mantlet of the Tiger II had 180mm. The war ended before it saw service.

T40 Tank Destroyer

The hull design was that of the M3 Lee/Grant, but the project was ended in 1942 when it was clear that there was an insufficient quantity of 3in guns available and the initial order for 1,000 vehicles was cancelled.

T57

Another American prototype that never reached service, the T57 self-propelled gun was a variant of another test vehicle, the T56. Both designs utilised the hull of the M3 Stuart light tank and a 3in gun, but the T57 was fitted with the Continental engine used in the M3 Lee medium tank.

Renault FT

Above: The two-man Renault FT entered service with the French Army in 1917; it was designed to "swarm" into German positions, and during World War I it proved very effective. During the inter-war years, FTs were purchased by 19 other nations, making it a highly influential vehicle.

Above right: French designers began work on the AMX 13 in 1946 and the first tanks entered service in 1953 with a 75mm gun. The distinctive design was conceived as a fast reconnaissance tank which was small and light enough to be air-portable. Production ceased in 1987 but the tank remains in service in many countries.

Right: The FCM36 was an expensive and poorly-armed two-man light tank that entered French service in 1938. One hundred tanks were delivered to the French army, and those that survived the fall of France in 1940 fell into German hands. Ten of these captured vehicles were fitted with 7.5cm PaK 40 anti-tank guns.

AMX 13 90

FCM36 Pak 40

Renault NC-31

Above: The famous Renault firm in France worked continuously during the inter-war years to develop various upgrades of their highly successful FT tank. The NC-2 (with the commercial name of NC-31) featured improved tracks and suspension to increase the speed of the tank. Several models were exported to China where they were deployed against Soviet and Japanese forces during the 1930s.

Type 59

Above: When it entered service the Chinese Type 59 was a simplified and cheaper version of the early model Soviet T-54 – many of its parts were interchangeable with its Soviet counterpart – and it remained in production until 1987. It has received several upgrades to its armour, armament and targeting systems and still forms the core of the armoured elements of the People's Liberation Army.

Crusader

The Crusader was developed in line with the British concept of the Cruiser tank – a quick, mobile vehicle to exploit breakthroughs in enemy positions. However, it was dogged by mechanical unreliability and thin armour and by mid-1943 it was regarded as obsolete.

Vickers Medium Mk I

The first modern tank to be built after the end of the World War I, the Vickers Mk I was poorly armoured but had a three-man turret, allowing the commander to spot targets and command the vehicle more effectively.

Sexton I

A very successful design of self-propelled gun using the chassis of the Canadian Ram medium tank with a British QF 25 pounder field gun, the Sexton I entered service in 1943. Its open hull offered little protection for the crew, but the gun was effective and reliable and could even be depressed to be used for direct fire.

FV3805

An experimental design of self-propelled gun, the FV3805 was tested between 1956 and 1960. Its hull was based on the Centurion main battle tank.

Tank, Infantry, Mk I (Churchill)

Above: Designed to support British infantry during World War II, the Mk I Churchill had a low top speed and heavy frontal armour – when it was introduced in 1941 only the Soviet KV-1 boasted better protection. The tracks of the Mk I were vulnerable to enemy fire, however, and the hull-mounted 75mm gun proved inefficient; as improved models were introduced, the Mk I was diverted to training duties or conversion to other roles.

Type 95 Ha-Gō

Above: The most numerous Japanese tank of World War II, the Ha-Go was designed as a fast, light tank with a three-man crew. It had a reliable 37mm gun and was relatively easy to maintain, but it was intended to be deployed against infantry rather than amoured vehicles. The appearance of the American M3 Lee and M4 Sherman in the Pacific rendered it obsolete.

THE TANK MUSEUM AND WORLD OF TANKS

Inspiration for the game comes from real tanks, many of which have been examined in great detail at the Tank Museum in England. The collaborative effort has led to a more accurate game and better preserved tanks. Curator David Willey tells us more about this special relationship...

The Tank Museum at Bovington in England has been around since 1923 – this was where tank crews trained with the new invention in World War I – and it is where the crews and their tanks came back to when the war was over. The Army has remained in this beautiful bit of countryside, training on tanks and armoured vehicles ever since. The collection began as a teaching aid to soldiers and over time has accumulated what is probably the most internationally comprehensive collection of armoured fighting vehicles in the world, housed in a vibrant museum and popular tourist attraction.

Different generations come to tanks in very different

EDUCATION ROOM

Fully sponsored by Wargaming, the Education Centre at The Tank Museum has seen some huge benefits since opening in 2012. It has allowed the Museum to welcome 7,000 school children each year and host community groups to take part in educational workshops. In the Education Room pupils learn about the history of tanks and are inspired by the science behind some iconic armoured vehicles.

ways – many visit the museum on holiday – it's a fantastic day out for the family, especially dads and sons; the smell of steel, canvas, oil and the look of these metal machines can be like catching a bug. The wartime generation is fast fading – but new family members want to find out what grandfather did in the war, the modeller who bought the kit

wants to see the real thing and for the last five years they have been joined, of course, by World of Tanks players.

Heresy though it may be to admit in this book I am not a player – but I am constantly amazed at the people who are. I have met soldiers who play regularly, staff who didn't think they'd like it but are now hooked, and children whose knowledge about the vehicles gained from the game is now astounding. The new audience the game brings in is very diverse in age, background and gender – and the way the game has brought a new level of interest to some of the more obscure areas of the collection is heartening. Who would have guessed that an obscure British tank experiment at the end of World War II would have young, female, World of Tanks vloggers swooning when they see it in the flesh (or steel, depending on your choice of idiom...)

As an independent charity the Tank Museum is always looking for ways to better meet its charitable aims – our job at the museum is to get the story of tank warfare to as wide an audience as possible. A games company that uses tanks

as a centrepiece for a hugely successful multi-million player game seems like a match made in heaven – but like any relationship it needs careful nurturing. The Museum is an obvious resource for the designers of the game. Having such a collection of vehicles to photograph, scan and, in many cases, see move, provides a fundamental body of material to help the makers give the game a sense of authenticity.

But the relationship has developed and goes much further. The Museum is also an obvious venue for Wargaming staff to meet their audience, so events have been held where players have had a chance to question the designers and staff and where 'winners' have been entertained and rewarded. There are of course the various forums and communities that spin out of such a project and here again the museum can host, entertain and add value to journalists, players, vloggers and staff.

In return the Tank Museum has benefitted by seeing its message delivered to many millions of players; the shared area of interest is tanks. It has received sponsorship from

FURY (2014)

Tracey Speight from the Special Projects team at World of Tanks opened the Museum's *Fury* exhibition. The Tank Museum had loaned it's Sherman tank to become 'Fury' in the film and had also loaned its Tiger tank to the set for two weeks. The story behind this project, the reasons the Museum got involved and the experiences of the staff on the set gave a potentially interesting exhibition for the Museum visitor. World of Tanks were able to make this happen by funding the exhibition, which opened the day after the film was released in UK cinemas.

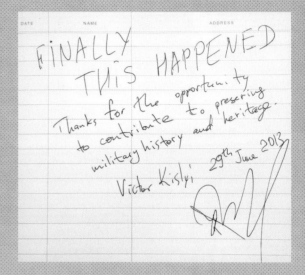

FINALLY THIS HAPPENED

Thanks for the opportunity to contribute to preserving military history and heritage.

Victor Kislyi 29th June 2013

World of Tanks to help with events such as the annual Tankfest, an exhibition on the Museum's involvement in the *Fury* film, to assist in the restoration of a number of the Museum's vehicles and to fit out its Education Room. New experiments in crowdsourcing captions for a huge photographic archive has begun and other exciting projects are on the way. At a more general level there is a massive number of people who have been drawn to the game and amongst these there are inevitably those who want to know more: what do these machines look like in reality, what was their actual use and why the differences in shape, weight, firepower, armour thickness, etc.

With these benefits to both parties and the players and those with an interest in tanks, long may the relationship continue.

DAVID WILLEY Curator, The Tank Museum

WORKSHOPS

The restoration of vehicles, some to running order and the conservation of others is a fundamental and ongoing task at the Museum. World of Tanks has helped fund some of these activities allowing the Museum to bring more vehicles back into public display. The Museum uses volunteers to help in the work and has won a number of awards for its partnership scheme where young offenders learn spanner and life skills in the workshop environment.

WORLD OF WARPLANES

World of Warplanes was announced only two months after World of Tanks was released in the West. The plan was to create a sister game to World of Tanks, in the air rather than on the ground, but with a shared economy so that players could easily switch between the two.

Two years ago it started its open beta, which still continues today. Much like World of Tanks that long beta is being used to refine and balance the game with constant feedback.

Like World of Tanks, World of Warplanes spans a rough period that starts in the inter-war years with biplane combat and ends up somewhere in the early Cold War with the introduction of the first jet fighters. It's a period at which air combat was at its most exciting, because computer assistance and long range missiles extended the range of combat and made dogfighting less important. Currently, six nations are represented: Germany, the Soviet Union, Japan, China, the UK and the U.S. Most planes stem from World War II, but there are a handful from 1920s and the 1950s.

The biggest difference between Warplanes and Tanks is the movement. Planes of course, move in three dimensions, not two. While World of Tanks plays much like a standard first person shooter, World of Warplanes has to offer an accessible version of flight controls while still working for the players who like to use an expensive joystick. Like the armour penetration mechanics of World of Tanks, the flight model of Warplanes is complex, but its complexity is hidden behind an easy to use arcade interface offering just enough assistance for players to quickly grasp how to fly while still feeling in control.

Another big difference is victory conditions. World of Tanks' base capturing doesn't make much sense in a dogfight, World of Warplanes instead includes ground

structures which can be damaged by dropping bombs or making strafing runs. Doing so fills up a 'supremacy' meter, as does destroying planes. Maxing out the supremacy meter or destroying all enemy planes results in victory. This opens up a lot of potential strategies, from a well escorted ground attack to an air supremacy force consisting entirely of agile fighters.

Much like World of Tanks there are several classes of plane. Fighters are light planes dedicated to air superiority, heavy fighters are less agile but have excellent weaponry, attack aircraft bomb ground targets and multi-role fighters do a little of everything. Lots of classic World War II fighters

are represented, such as the British Spitfire, the German Messerschmitt and the Soviet IL series.

Even within the fighters there are very different approaches. They can be broadly broken down into aircraft that rely on making tight horizontal turns (turnfighters) and those that rely on vertical manoeuvres ('boom and zoom' fighters). The latter are built to exploit the third dimension, climbing high above the battlefield and going into steep dives to attack the enemy, most heavy fighters will use "boom and zoom" tactics. There are also some fighters that can do a little of both, beating "boom and zoom" fighters on the turn and turnfighters on the vertical.

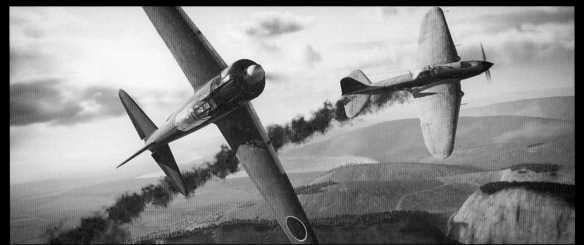

Switching between World of Warplanes and World of Tanks is easy, because they share the same economy. Specifically gold, free experience and premium time are shared between the two games, while credits are not. This allows veteran tank players (which you might well be if you've made it this far through the book!) to get a jump start in World of Warplanes by using their free experience to progress quickly through the lower levels.

Experienced tank players will find World of Warplanes a home away from home. After a particularly slow game of tanks it can be incredibly refreshing to leap into the cockpit and head into a dogfight, confident in the fact that there is no where to hide up in the sky. Meanwhile, you'll still be racking up vital experience that can benefit either game.

WORLD OF WARSHIPS

World of Warships is the third game in Wargaming's 'World of' series, based on the slow pace and big, big guns of naval combat. In a way it's returning to that early inspiration for World of Tanks, Navy Field (see more about that on page 19).

World of Warships is currently in the early stages of an open beta which, judging by Wargaming's previous record, we can expect to last some time.

One big difference Tanks players are likely to notice in Warships is the scale. An entire company of Tanks would very easily fit aboard a World of Battleships aircraft carrier. The maps are huge too, which is understandable considering that these ships are packing guns whose range is measured in scores of miles.

While Wargaming have enhanced ship speed to the extent that battles can be over in 15 minutes rather than a few hours, the game still runs at a much slower pace than Tanks or Warplanes. Guns and torpedoes take time to travel to their targets, and even more time to reload, and ships swing in lazy arcs. It's slow but purposeful, making the hits feel all the more devastating when they finally connect. This also places a lot of evidence on planning your manoeuvres ahead of time, and the game even offers the ability to set waypoints for your ship to automatically follow, real time strategy style.

Like Warplanes and Tanks there are several different styles of ships to choose from. Destroyers are the glass cannons of the seas. They are fast, manoeuvrable and carry powerful torpedoes, allowing them to hunt the much larger Battleships. Cruisers are mid-size ships that can fill a variety of roles, specializing in either big guns, torpedoes or anti-aircraft to counter different types of ship. Battleships are large heavily armoured ships that can equip massive cannons and huge amount of anti-aircraft guns, but need to be protected from fast moving aircraft and destroyers. Finally, there are aircraft carriers, the most unusual of the classes, taking an almost real time strategy approach by projecting power at a distance with squadrons of fighter

planes, dive bombers and torpedo bombers, but are vulnerable if caught in ship to ship combat. One thing we won't likely be seeing is submarines, which the developers are currently eschewing because, although historically accurate, they're not very fun to play with or against.

World of Warships will eventually boast same shared economy as Warplanes and Tanks, but at the time of writing it is still using alternative currency during testing. It should provide a very different experience to Warplanes' fast paced air combat and Tanks' more traditional FPS, for those days when players want to participate in a slower, more strategic experience.